Chess for Beginners:

Understand the Rules, Board, Pieces and Effective Openings: Choose Your Strategy and Start Winning

George J. Stevens

TABLE OF CONTENT

PART ONE: PLAYING THE CHESS GAME

The chess piece

The King

The Queen

The Knight

The Bishop

The Pawn

How to set up the chess pieces

Best chess strategy

Best chess openings

The Queen Gambit Declined

Chess tactics

Secrets of the middle game

Bad chess opening moves

Chess endgames

How to decide your next chess move

PART TWO: HISTORY OF THE CHESS GAME

History of the chess game

Development of theory

The time element and competition

INTRODUCTION

If you are reading this book, chances are that you would like to get better at chess. Are you a beginner at chess and want to improve your skills? Have you dived into the wide world of chess, but are not sure how to win against your opponents? Have you played some tournaments without enjoying satisfying results? We hope to have a solution for you in this book. You will see that in order to get better at chess, far more is needed than just sitting in front of books for hours or learning certain patterns by heart.

Most beginners wrongly think that imitating grandmasters or memorizing their moves, even without understanding them, is the key to success. However, they are wrong. Those things alone do not really help you to improve at all.

There are concepts and precepts to chess, and all you need is a well organized guide. This will ensure you learn right from what the chess board looks like, the chess pieces and what moves they can perform.

This book hopes to simplify and effortlessly enable you to understand, practice and enjoy the chess game. To this end, the book "chess for beginners" begins by explaining all rudiments of chess and finally giving you an historical overview of the game. Every chapter and phase of this book engage you with practice from well set of pictorial guide.

After you learn how the chess pieces move, you should learn how to find the best square for each piece. This will help you to play better chess and win more games. Further included in this book, is how you start, control and end a chess game. All grandmaster would have graced the chess game always knowing exactly how to gain control of a game and kill it off. As a chess beginner, this could be daunting and could take lot of time to understand. However, this guide would do justice to you enabling you to become the best you can be in chess game.

You learn moves, unlearn and then relearn them, and you will see what the grandmaster does in particular situation.

THE CHESS PIECE

THE KING

The king is the most important piece in any chess game and is positioned next to the queen, wearing a cross on his head. He is worth infinite pawns, the lives of all your other pieces and when you checkmate the opponent's king, the game is over and you take home a win. Thus it is important to keep your king secure and try to weaken the opponents'. The king is constrained in his movement. He can move only one square in either direction, but only if he is not put in check by doing so. Besides, this square must not be occupied by any other of your pieces (only one piece can ever occupy a square). The king will engage in a special move called "castling". When you castle, you simultaneously move your king and one of your rooks.

The king is the piece with a cross atop. Although this may not be the most powerful piece in chess, it is definitely the most important. If you are losing your king you have lost the game. You want to make sure you defend your king at the start of the game. The king can become a very strong ally in your offence later in the game so be prepared to use it.

The kings start on the e1 and e8 squares. The white king should be on a dark square. The black king starts on a light square.

OVERVIEW

On the e1 square, the white chess king starts and on the e8 square, the black king starts. This ought to be the king's opposite color. If the square of e1 is white, then the board must be rotated so that the square of e1 is black.

Movement

The king can move one square anywhere. It cannot hop over the other pawns so there is no legal move for the king to make at the start of a chess game as it is surrounded by other pieces. When a king moves to a square, you will see Ke5. The K is the king, and e5 is the square it moves to. If the king catches a piece on e5 you can see the notation written Kxe5. The x indicates a fragment caught. The one disadvantage the king has when moving is that it cannot move to a square invaded by pieces of an enemy. In e.g. as you can see, Kxe4 can take the rook on e4 since another piece does not protect the rook. However, the king cannot take the knight on b4 because the rook defends that square.

The king can move one square in any direction as indicated.

The king can take the rook, because it is not defended. It cannot take the knight because it is defended.

The king moves from d4 to e5. This move would be notated as Ke5.

Castling movement by the king.

The king can join a special move called "castling." When you castle, you move your king and one of your rooks. You move the king two squares to your rook and then move the rook to the square where the king crossed (be sure to do it in this order – if you move your rook first it is counted as a normal rook move and you will lose the chance to castle). There are two castling types in chess:

- Castling on the kingside (often called castling short)
- Castling on the queenside (often called castling long)

Castling might sound complicated in theory, but let's see how easy it is in practice:

1.

Starting position for illustration.

2.

White piece castles to the kingside.

3.

Black piece castles to the queenside

However, there are a number of rules when castling is possible and when not. You can only castle, if:

1. Your king has not moved in the game yet.
2. Your king is not in check.
3. The king does not castle through a square which is controlled by an opponent's piece.
4. The king is not in check after castling.
5. The rook has not been moved in the game yet.

Reasons for castling

All beginners are taught castling early in their games. The instructor says this as a rule and can also clarify the value of casting like to secure your king." However, why is this the case? Let's look deeper into castling in chess and you may be surprised at some of the new ideas you are learning.

First of all, the main two reasons for castling in chess are:

GETTING THE KING OUT OF THE CENTER

Remember that the first reason we are talking about is not "getting the king safe," but it is actually "getting the king out of the center." Just because you castled it does not mean the king is instantly magically safe. There may be times when storm clouds brew over our kingside, and the pieces of our adversary aim in that direction, and it would be a massive mistake to castle kingside, taking our king straight into a major assault.

Not the main thing is keeping the king out of the middle. Most castling will secure your king. However, that is just because a king is not usually protected in the middle of the board, where pieces from the queenside, kingside and center can easily strike it. Castling long limits the king to one side of the board. Make sure the role you are able to deal with is an improvement. Often a king can be perfectly safe in the center of the board, without castling at all.

Let's look at the place to the right. Should the black castle be in this position? General principles would have said, "Of course! Black must be castled so that his king is protected." But does the castling in this example really make our king safer than keeping

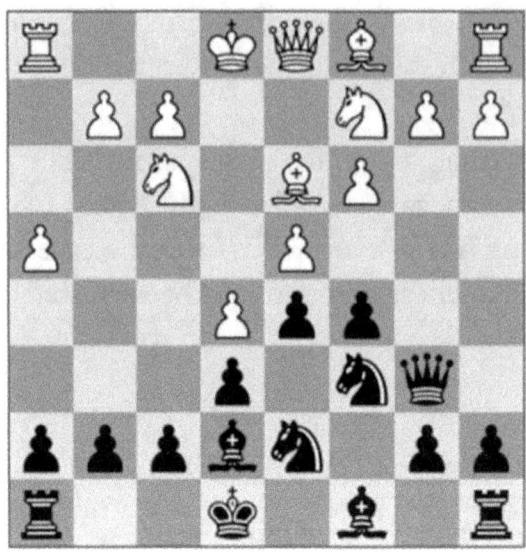 him in the center of the board? Well not this time, man. If we castled right now, white could actually launch a matching attack with the Bxh7+ move! Our king would have been much better sitting in the middle of the board at the moment, compared to castling the king's side right away and being killed.

Activating a Rook

The second explanation for the castle is to activate our fortress. By its design, the castle flips the king and rooks so that the ring is closer to the middle of the board. Without this move being possible in chess, it would be even more difficult to activate the rings, so we would have to manually walk the king out of the center of the board, and then place our rings in the center. Without the castling, it will take a lot longer.

When we do castle, we put a ring closer to the middle where it can be used for several different things, such as defending a main central pawn, manipulating an open file, and assaulting the enemy king (who sits in the center of the board because he hasn't castled it yet!). Castling and triggering a ring is also very important when we are on the way to growth. This helps us to get another piece into the game faster and attack our opponent more quickly.

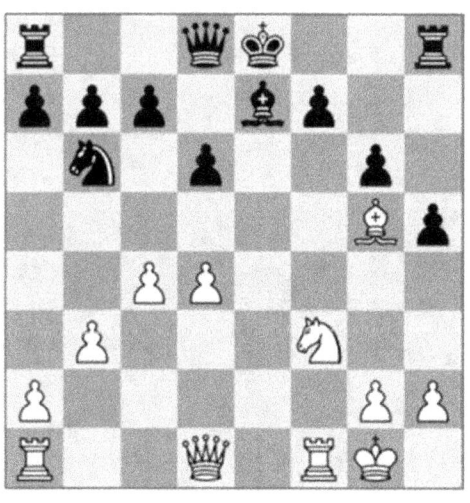

In a spot to the right, white has made a move or two earlier and has the chance to use his rook to strike black's uncastled king. With the moves Bxe7 followed by Re1, or only doing Re1 and pinning the bishop first, white is using his newly activated rook very well in the assault on the king of black. Now that we have a better understanding of the logic behind castling, we will be better prepared to use it in our own games at the right time.

Remember, the castle cannot be undone! You have to deal with the effects of a change (good or bad) once you have made it.

THE QUEEN

The queen is a piece with a crown on the end, but not a cross. This is the strongest piece of chess which incorporates the movements of both the rook and the bishop. Like the rook, it is considered a big piece of chess.

The queen, besides the king, is the chess game's most important and strong piece. Every player has only one queen, it worth 9 pawns!

The queen sits next to the bishop on the central square, the color of the piece (a black queen starts on the black square in the middle of all the other pieces, a white queen on a white square).

Overview

Queens start on d1 and d8 squares. This should be the queen's color. If you see the d1 square is a dark square, you need to rotate the board so the d1 square is a light square. Using the queen correctly is one of chess' most critical parts.

The queen is strong, so you want to use it, but if it is not protected your opponent can capture your queen and lead to a fast loss. The queen is worth 9 points, more than a combined

bishop and rook.

The queen starts right next to the king. They should be on the d1 and d8 squares.

Movement

The queen incorporates bishop-rook motions. It can move some squares diagonally, or go up, down and sideways as many squares without jumping over another piece. When a queen moves, you normally see notation as Qh4. The Q is the queen, and h4 is the square the queen moves to. If the queen captures a piece on h4, Qxh4 will be noted.

The queen can move vertically, horizontally, or diagonally any number of squares.

The queen moves to the d5 square and is notated Qd5.

As she has the widest scope of all pieces, she can become your opponents' most dangerous game member. Protecting her and simultaneously using her efficiently is necessary. For most matches, queen's loss means the whole game's loss. So be careful with your queen as she is peculiar. She can move in any direction and squares. She cannot just leap over other chess piece. The queen can catch any piece in the opponent's direction. This piece is useful for various techniques and attacks. Be careful not to open your queen too fast as you find her in danger from the opponent's pieces.

One of the biggest errors beginners make with their queens is getting them to play too early. They think they should get them involved in the fight early because they are the strongest. This sounds good, but technically it does not work. Players who get their queens out early typically lose time in growth. Your opponent can concentrate on developing his pieces toward the center when you are worried about your queen's defense.

At the beginning of a game, the queen seldom does much harm. However, mixed with bishops, knights, and rooks, the queen does much harm. When designing your queen early, make sure it supports as many pieces as possible. So when any of your pieces starts an attack, your queen will be there helping the attack, but not in threat. Early in a chess game, you usually do not want to move your queen much. It helps your pawns, bishops, and knights. As you enter the middle game (about 15 moves into the game), the queen will start getting more involved and playing more offence.

THE KNIGHT

The knight is the horse-like piece. It is the most difficult piece to describe, since it has a peculiar movement. The knight, worth 3 points, is considered a minor piece. It is usually considered as powerful as a bishop, but for specific reasons. Although both pieces are worth 3 points, the knight will rule supreme in certain positions. The two knights, looking like little ponies, are the chess game's minor pieces. Initially, they are inside the rooks and their worth is equal to 3 pawns.

This chess piece, often called "horse", has a very mysterious way of moving on the board that can puzzle beginners to learn the rules of chess. The knight is the only piece that can hop over pieces.

Each side starts with two knights. They should be placed on b1/g1 for white and b8/g8 for black.

You are start out with two knights. They will be between your rook and bishops on white squares b1/g1 and b8/g8 black.

Movement

The knight is the only piece that can hop over another piece. The knight has a leg on the queen, but controls less total squares than the queen does. Knight's movement can be called an L. You can think of it as a two-one approach. This means that the knight can move two squares up/down/sideways, followed by one square to make an L, or move one square up/down/sideways to make an L. Look at the example C to see a knight's potential squares. As described before the knight can also leap over stuff. This means that even though the knight is surrounded by stuff, it can still move to the same number of squares (assuming another piece you own does not occupy the final destination).

Example C: The knight moves in an L shape. It is the only piece that can hop over another piece.

Since the knight can jump over pieces, the possible moves are not limited even if the knight is surrounded.

The knight is the only piece besides the pawn that can move on the very first move in the game.

If the knight moves, the notation will be Ne4. The N represents the knight (the king takes K), and e4 represents the square it moves to. If two knights can move to the same square, then you would see Nd2e4. This means the d2 knight moved to e4 instead of another knight that could also move to e4.

It moves over squares in L-shape. This means that this chess piece first moves two squares in one direction (left, right, back, or forward) and then one square in horizontal or vertical. If that sounds complicated, do not worry because the diagram will help you out. Of course, it is also possible to move backwards in the same form – the knight will move one square in either direction (but not diagonally) first then two squares across or down. Try drawing a three-square L-shaped finger on the paper.

This special piece can only move to eight squares in the centre of the board. Although the knight cannot cover as many squares as other pieces, it is very useful in your games for different tactical reasons.

This makes this chess piece remarkably precious. Knights are often much more useful in the center of the floor. Knights generally do not do well at the edge of the chess board, and they certainly do not do well at the corner of the chess board. Make sure you still have your knights at the middle of the board. It is also important to note that knights should be the first pieces you have made. Knights in production should come after pawns.

THE BISHOP

The bishop is not as powerful as the rook, and is called a minor piece. It can still cover more ground and operates in pairs. Both bishops are the game's other minor pieces. They sit beside the knights and like the knights, worth 3 pawns each (some grandmasters would value them at about 3.3 pawns due to how powerful they can be in open positions). Happily, bishops' movement, originally called elephants, is much simpler than the knight. The bishop ruler of chess board diagonals. One is light-squared, the other dark-squared.

Start with two bishops. They are right next to the king and queen. You will get one bishop on light squares and one bishop on dark squares. The bishop piece will remain on the same color square. The bishop is worth 3 points in a knight's chess game.

Each side starts with two bishops.

One bishop will be on a light square and one on a dark square.

How the bishop moves

The bishop can move as many squares as he likes, without jumping over another piece. When a bishop moves you will see a notation like Be4. The B is the bishop, and e4 is the square it moves to. If the bishop catches a pawn on e4, it is written as Bxe4. At the start of the game, bishops are blocked by pawns, but you normally move your pawns early. The door opens to include the bishops in the game. Bishops will be one of your key pieces in the early game to attack your opponent.

Bishops can move diagonally.

Any number of   bishops are initially blocked by pawns but will be one of the first piece you move

Squares without jumping over another piece.

When no other pieces are in their path, bishops can move diagonally in any direction as many squares as desired. They can grab any piece along the diagonals and as they can reach so many squares (they can move in one move from one end of the board to the other), they can be very useful particularly when operating in tandem.

It is also necessary to remember that a bishop can never leave the starting color square. That means that two bishops typically work together very well, since they can cover the whole board with a small number of moves if they are not blocked. Although bishops are worth the same as knights, many people prefer bishops early in a game as most games open. Once the game continues, if the game begins to close and the board gets crowded, then players prefer knights.

Make sure you do not trap your bishops if you have them and make sure they are used to their full capacity.

THE ROOK

The rook is the castle-like piece. The rook is a very powerful piece, often called a major piece, and is only outranked by the queen. At the start of any game, you have 2 tower-like pieces in the chess board corners. In chess we call them rooks. A rook is a very valuable piece worth 4 to 5 pawns and has a wide scope. Every side begins with two rooks in the board's four corners. Rooks worth 5 chess points. Although points do not tell the whole story in a chess game, there is some measure of how solid a piece is. If you give up a 3-point chess piece in return for your opponents rook, that is a fair deal for you.

Each side starts with two rooks placed on the four corners of the chess board.

The rook's movement

The rook can move squares up, down, and across the chess board. It cannot hop over other pieces, so it cannot move at the start of chess game.

At game start, the rook is surrounded by a pawn and a knight. One mistake beginners make is never unleashing the rook into the game. The rook rarely gets involved early in the game but you need to find a way to use the rook later in the game, or you will lose your best pieces contributing to the game.

 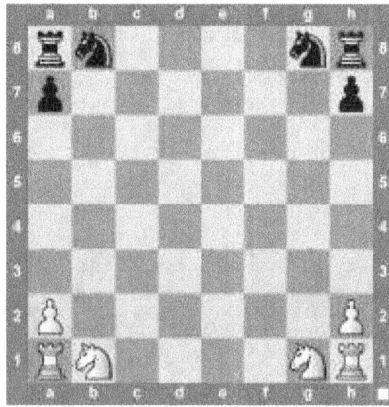

The rook can move vertically or horizontally any number of squares without jumping over another piece.

At the beginning of the game the rook is blocked in by the pawn and knight.

Both rooks can move to e4. Since the rook on d1 moves to d4 the chess notation would be Rd1d4.

When a rook moves, you will see notation like Re4. The R represents a rook moving to represent the square to which the rook moves. If the rook captures material on e4 square, the notation is Rxe4. It is also common for two rooks to move to the same square. Notation will then be Re1e4. That implies that the e1 rook moves to e4. This is to limit any other rook uncertainty that might also shift to e4.

The key thing you need to know about rooks is that they operate best on open files, making the rooks even stronger vertically and horizontally if there are no pieces in the way. The rooks are just as strong as the amount of squares or pieces they can support. A common mistake people make is not triggering their rooks. When creating your pieces, you should try to move all your pieces to the middle, and after caslting for king protection, make sure your rooks are always on open files. If you lose a pawn, make sure you put a rook on that file. If chess players use their rooks more effectively, they would immediately become much better players.

Bottom line

Chess piece movement is the simplest to learn from all pieces—rooks can go forward, backward, left or right. Naturally, in the same leap, the rook cannot change directions. As long as no other piece is in their path, they cannot leap over pieces; they can move any number of squares in the direction chosen.

THE PAWN

The pawn is the basic chess piece, and each side begins with eight of them. Every pawn is worth 1 point. Although that might not seem a lot, if they have a 1-point advantage, many good chess players will win a chess game.

Arrangement

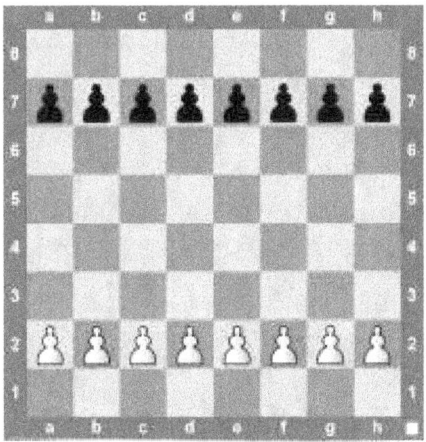

Each side starts with 8 pawns.

Overview

Although the pawn is the board's weakest piece, it serves a critical game position. Most of the early part of the game will concentrate on the pawn structure, controlling the board center with your pawns. The other pieces are going to help the pawn in the early stages. Later on the pawns will play a more supporting position for the minor and major pieces by limiting the squares to which the opponent will go.

At the beginning of the game, each player has 8 pawns before the other 8 pieces. The pawn is one of the game's most underrated chess pieces because it is pretty little, and you have got plenty on the chess board. However, that is a fatal mistake; some famous chess players call them "the chess soul". For example, one explanation is that when they enter the other side of the board, they can turn into any other piece but the king. Pawns have fewest movement options. On their first move, they can go one or two squares forward. A pawn will go one square straight on all other moves. The exception is when pawns grab the opponent's chess pieces – then move forward one square diagonally. Moreover one exceptional rule for pawn moves is called "en passant".

Pawns' movement

The pawn is the only piece on the chess board that cannot go backwards. It is also the only piece where you cannot move it the same number of squares the whole game. The first time you move a pawn you can move it one or two squares. If the pawn has moved you can only move it one square after that.

Pawns only move forward.

On its 1st move, you can move 1 or 2 squares.

After the pawn has moved it can only move forward one square for the rest of the game.

Another difference is that when the pawn goes forward it cannot grab another piece right in front of it. It can only capture a piece diagonally, so it cannot move diagonally unless it is capturing a piece. Look at the example D and you can see that the pawn on d5 cannot take the pawn on d6 (located directly in front of it) (located directly in front of it). Instead the only move the pawn can make is to take the pawn on e6.

When a pawn moves, you will see e5. This is unusual if you do not see a letter stating what piece moves. If you just see a square, the pawn moves there. If a d5 pawn captures an e6 pawn, you would see the exd6 notation.

Example D: Pawns can only capture diagonally. It **cannot** capture a piece directly in front of it.

Bottom-line

When starting the game, you should concentrate on two things when moving your pawns. The first thing you can always do is gain center control. Many players believe d and e pawns are the most important since they usually control the board center. These pawns are typically formed early. The second thing you need to worry about in a chess game is king defense. Most players castle kingside, so it is suggested you do not move the pawns if you do not have to. The more you step away from your king, the less secure the king becomes.

One of the pawn's greatest advantages is that if they reach the 8th rank (the other side of the board), they can be promoted or traded for any piece on the board except the king and cannot remain a pawn. This is extremely important because a player can convert a pawn into a queen and change the whole game.

THE EN PASSANT MOVE

The en-passant pawn capture rule is a special pawn move rarely known to beginning chess players. Even older players can easily overlook it. There is only a special move a pawn can make in passing. This can only happen immediately after a pawn moves two squares. If you have a pawn next to the pawn after moving two squares, you can take this pawn with en passant, but only one move. Any other move you make would deny the possibility of en passant.

Rule 3.7.d, from the chess rule book stats that "A pawn attacking a square crossed by an opponent's pawn which has advanced two squares in one move from its original square may capture this opponent's pawn as though the latter had been moved only one square. This capture is only legal on the move following this advance and is called an '"en passant' capture."

You cannot read such a boring, technical summary. By reading official rules, nobody learns chess, cover-to-cover. That is like reading the manual before trying to assemble a piece of furniture! As we all know, most of us ignore long reading material and simply dive in (sometimes with disastrous results). Starting in chess, we learn how various pieces move. Some are simple – bishops move diagonally, rooks move vertically and horizontally, queens have all these powers.

Knights are trickier with their "L" movement and jumping ability. Pawns, the weakest soldiers, are even harder; they usually move one square ahead, except when they can move two squares, but when they catch, they do this diagonally!

After a while it becomes second nature, but to anyone first entering the game, special cases like en passant may be gaps in information. Even a chess teacher may neglect mentioning en passant to avoid confusing their student while trying to explain more general, simple concepts.

The conditions for en passant are:

- The capturing pawn must be on its fifth rank (imagine a white pawn on d5).

- The threatened pawn must have moved two squares from its starting square, and be on an adjacent file (so, if white has a pawn on d5, then black's c-pawn and e-pawn could be threatened with en passant capture if they move from their starting squares).

- The capture can only be made on the move immediately after the opposing pawn makes the move; otherwise, the right to capture en passant is lost.

Ex. E&F show en passant. White has moved d4. Black has a c4 pawn and one move to play cxd3. It is an odd move as the black pawn does not end up on a square occupied by a white piece, but it actually captures the white pawn on d4. This generally ends with a puzzled opponent if they have never seen it, but you can direct them to this site if you need to prove it is a legal pass.

Example E: White just moved to d4.
Black on the next move can capture the white pawn by playing cxd3.
Black can capture with en passant.

Why did the rule-makers see fit to add the exception to the way pawns usually move?

In the early days of chess (over 500 years ago), a pawn could not move two squares forward on the first move. The first two-square transfer rule was introduced to speed up the game, but it resulted in a loss for the player whose pawn had made it 5th.

Without moving by, pawns in 5th rank could be moved by enemy pawns advancing two squares, with no chance of capture. The en passant capture was brought in to avoid pawns moving ahead of two squares from being caught by 5th-rank pawns, as if they had passed only one square.

In most places, though allowing the pawn to move two squares on its first move, the en passant rule was adopted. Together, they represent two of the last big changes in chess law as the game originated from India.

Why should you play en passant?

You can only play en passant as you judge it to be the best move open to you. I saw beginning players confidently playing to show off that they know the rule, only to see their position crumble. Somehow, they feel they have to, if they can play en passant. It is a mistake. Because of its relative anonymity, some consider playing against a relatively new chess player "unsporting". If your opponent just gets the hang of playing chess, it seems a trifle unfair whisking off the board when they were not expecting it.

If it is a friendly game, you may try to warn your opponent about the possibility of playing en passant and encourage them to take back their move, but better remember the lesson if you are not so merciful. After all it is a chess rule, even if a little obscure.

Personally, I would not hesitate to play, even if my opponent did not know. One learns more from losing than winning, and you should never hesitate to teach your challenger a lesson.

Overview of how chess pieces move

Kings move one square in any direction, so long as that square is not attacked by an enemy piece. Additionally, kings are able to make a special move, known as castling.

Queens move diagonally, horizontally, or vertically any number of squares. They are unable to jump over pieces.

Rooks move horizontally or vertically any number of squares. They are unable to jump over pieces. Rooks move when the king castles.

Bishops move diagonally any number of squares. They are unable to jump over pieces.

Knights move in an 'L' shape': two squares in a horizontal or vertical direction then move one square horizontally or vertically. They are the only piece able to jump over other pieces.

Pawns move one square vertically, with the option to move two squares if they have not yet moved. Pawns are the only piece caught differently than they move. Pawns grab one square diagonally forward. Pawns cannot withdraw on captures or moves. After reaching the other side of the board, a pawn promotes every other piece, except a king. Additionally, pawns will make the en passant special move.

Everyone in the world knows the popular chess board game. However, many people glance at the chess board and feel utterly frustrated, believing it is just a game for incredibly smart people and a game they will never understand. They look at the chess board, see 32 chess pieces they do not know the names of, and have no idea what to do with them.

If you are curious about chess, we want to end your frustration and show you that learning to play chess is not scary.

The chess board consists of 64 squares, half white half black. Each player has 6 different types of pieces: 8 pawns, 2 rooks, 2 knights, 2 bishops; the queen, and the king are the most important. At the beginning of the game, we find 32 pieces on the chess board, half white and half black. They all occupy half of the entire chess board and each side attempts to use them effectively to checkmate the opponent's king.

Choosing the best square and activating the best moves for chess pieces.

After learning how chess pieces move, learn how to find the best square for each piece. This will make you play better and win more games. True, the "best square" for each piece will change many times during a chess game, but there are some general rules that will be useful in most of your games.

During a chess game, our pieces can occupy several squares. However, some of these squares are usually better.

There are many reasons why a piece is better positioned on one square than another is-

- Better mobility.
- Safety.
- Control over other pieces or squares.
- Attacking influence.

For instance, in the diagram below, white's bishops are in very different circumstances.

The light-squared bishop is on a good square and the dark bishop is on a bad square.

The light-squared bishop will move to multiple squares, while the dark-squared bishop is stuck behind his own pawns. With nothing in the place, it is basically the same as if it wasn't on the board at all. The light-squared bishop will run free across the board.

MORE EXAMPLES

The blockading knight

Knight is our opponent's best piece to block risky advancing pawns. Since it controls a handful of squares in all directions, the knight is the ideal piece to prevent pawns going forward.

Blockading knight

The white knight prevents the black pawn on d4 from advancing in the diagram above and the pawn on the c-file cannot simply advance because the knight will catch everything when defending the d3 square.

Another case for white would be if the d3 square had a rook instead of a knight.

Bad rook

In the diagram above the black pawn on the c-file will eventually attack the rook and take possession of the d3 square, connect the pawns and ultimately get promoted.

The safe king

When the game begins, the king is in the middle. That is not a good square for your biggest piece. Your opponent can easily target the king and in a few moves build a powerful assault.

That is why the king's best position is normally tucked away on the g-file after short castles.

Good king and bad king

The centralized rook

The key concept here is exactly the opposite of the last case!

In the starting position, the rooks are on the sides, but the best squares are in the middle.

In the diagram below, white rooks are on their best squares, while black rooks are on the worst squares.

When the rooks are centralized, they help the other pieces' function in trying to manage the board's center. You can also see the rooks in the diagram above on the same files as black's queen and king. This is important because when the center opens, these rooks strike the opponent's two most important pieces.

Centralized rooks

The active queen

The queen is the board's most flexible, strongest piece. That is why our queen still has plenty of space for long maneuvers. We should also always strive to keep our opponent's queen under control without jumping around and causing problems.

This is an example of very active queen (white) vs. a very passive queen (black):

Good queen vs. bad queen

The useful pawns

"The pawns are the soul of chess: are they alone that determine the attack and the defense, and the winning or losing of the game depends entirely on their good or bad arrangement." – Philidor

There are some universal pawn-playing rules. For instance, you always want to link your pawns. There are several exceptions where advanced players prefer to play with isolated pawns, but we won't concentrate on this advanced definition. For now, knowing a pawn is the best thing to defend another pawn is enough.

In the diagram below, you can see how white's pawns are connected and supporting each other, but black's pawns are far from each other, therefore they are weak.

Good pawns vs. bad pawns

Another important general rule is always trying to keep the opponent from 'passing pawns.' A passed pawn is a pawn that the opponent's pawns cannot stop from advancing, so it becomes highly dangerous as it has a direct path to eighth rank.

Passed pawn

In the diagram above, the black pawn cannot be stopped and it will continue moving forward until it promotes.

All chess pieces often have one or two squares appropriate at any given time. This can change during a chess game, but we should be aware of universal rules if we want to take our chess to next level. Knowing which squares are best for your pieces will give you an advantage over your rivals. It makes proper defense or setting up fantastic attacks. This is a guide for beginners who already know chess basic rules.

HOW TO SET UP THE CHESS PIECES

The chess board and chess pieces

Each player has 8 pawns at the beginning of a chess game. Pawns are the least important chess pieces on the chessboard. Although you are still an amateur, it is no real drama if you lose one of the pawns during the game.

Each player also has 4 minor pieces at the beginning of a game – two knights and two bishops each. Knights and bishops are worth about 3 pawns. Moreover each player has two rooks which are more valuable chess pieces, being worth 5 pawns.

The queen, the second tallest chess piece on the chess board, is the second precious piece of the game. Each player has one queen who is extremely powerful and worth 9 pawns. Do you see how valuable she is? She is worth more than all the pawns which you hold.

The most critical chess piece is the king! You must care about his safety in the entire game – or you will lose the game. Chess game's main objective is to checkmate the king.

So while attacking your opponent's king, yours must always be in a safe position, covered by other pieces. Your king's worth cannot be measured in pawns because it would be infinite.

Before we set up chess boards, let's look at the chess board layout itself. The chessboard has 64 squares.

Half of the squares are white and the other half is black, spaced uniformly. Half of the chess pieces are white, while the other half is black.

The outline of the chess board consists of 8 horizontal lines (called ranks) and 8 vertical lines (called files).

Horizontal lines are shown by numbers from 1 to 8 and vertical lines with letters a to h.

Consequently, a number and a letter fit each square, making it easier to understand where the chess pieces are positioned.

If you are the player with white pieces, at the beginning of the game, your chess pieces will be on the first two ranks – lines 1 and 2.

Whereas, if you are the player with the black pieces, your chess pieces will be on the last two ranks at the start of the game, lines 7 and 8.

From white's perspective, the chess board without chess pieces looks like the right picture.

Here's a useful tip to make sure your chessboard is oriented correctly: "white on the right". If the bottom right square is white, your chessboard is facing the right way.

Here are the steps to follow to set a chess board correctly:

Step 1: Make sure the board is in the correct position.

Positioning a chess board is the first step. The chess board usually has letters and numbers, players should always sit with the letters on the board side. Ensure the bottom-right corner is a light-colored square.

Step 2: place the rooks into the corners.

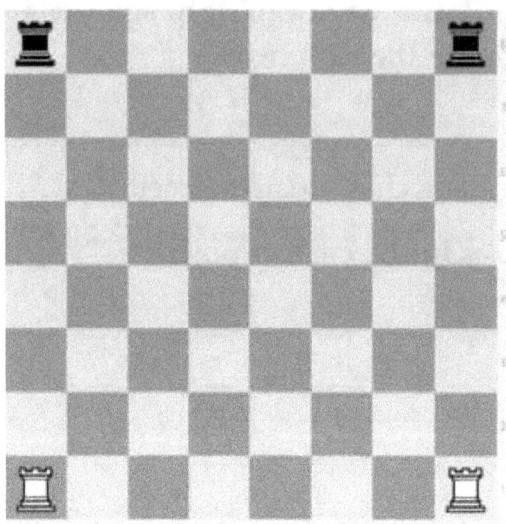

Rooks typically look like towers in most chess sets designs. These bits still go in the corners, much like a fortress castle. Looking at the coordinates it should be a1, h1, a8, and h8.

Step 3: knights should always go alongside rooks.

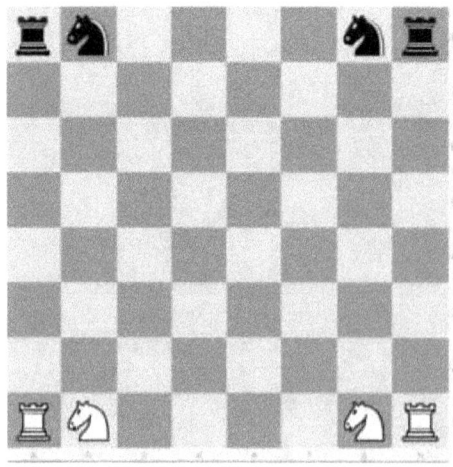

Knights are next in line to rooks when setting a chess board. Knights typically portray a horse as a real knight might ride. Know, knights defend a castle walls. They are in "L" form. They are worth around 3 pawns and are particularly useful at game start due to their unique ability to hop over other pieces.

Step 4: The bishops go next to the knights.

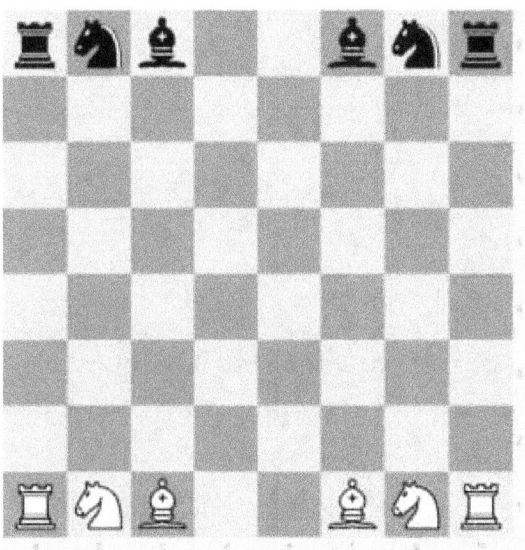

Bishops are the third piece on the back row when setting the chess board. Bishops move some unblocked squares diagonally. The bishops' name helps you remember their place. Typically a religious figure handles a coronation of a real-life king or queen, who places the crown on top of the new monarch's head.

Bishops are thought worth around 3 pawns in chess. They are mostly active at game start, but if they survive in the late game they gain additional power due to their long range.

Step 5: the queen goes to her own color square.

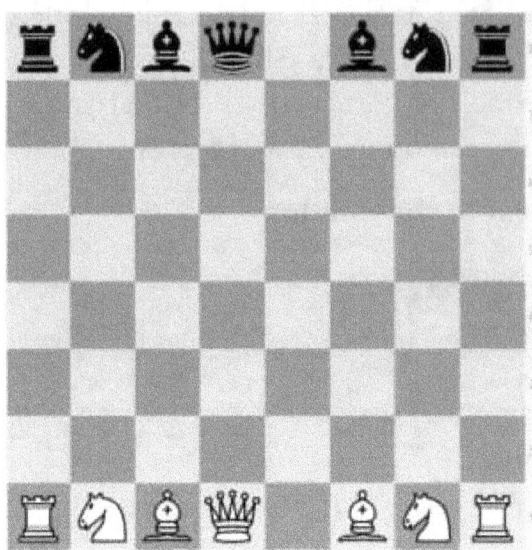

Now the first row should have two squares left. The queen is positioned on the color square representing the player it represents, so the white queen is on a light square and the black queen is on a dark square. A nice way to note that queens, being royal, want their dress to match their shoes. Queens can move any number of unblocked squares horizontally, vertically, or diagonally – combining rook and bishop forces. Theoretically, queens worth around 9 pawns.

Step 6: The king goes on the last square remaining.

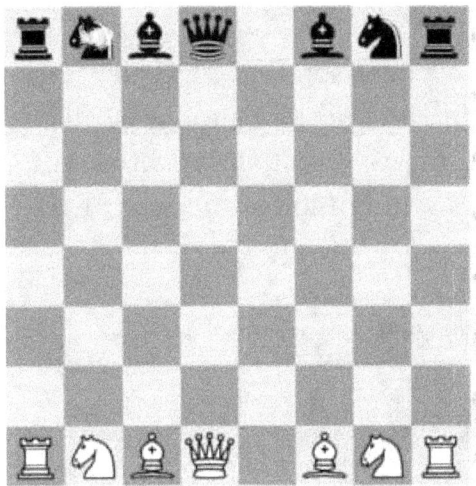

Finally, each player should have one square left on the first board. Place the king there. The king can move one square anywhere. The ultimate aim of the game is to "checkmate" the opponent's king, while not losing your own so kings are worth more than all the other pieces on the board put together, but not as good in play. Your king is saved at all costs.

Step 7: Put all eight pawns in second and seventh ranks in front of all other pieces.

Each color has eight pawns in a chess set. They are the least valuable piece. Every square in the second row should be filled with colored pawns. By placing the pawns on the board first you can easily locate the other pieces and complete the rest of the chess board setup steps.

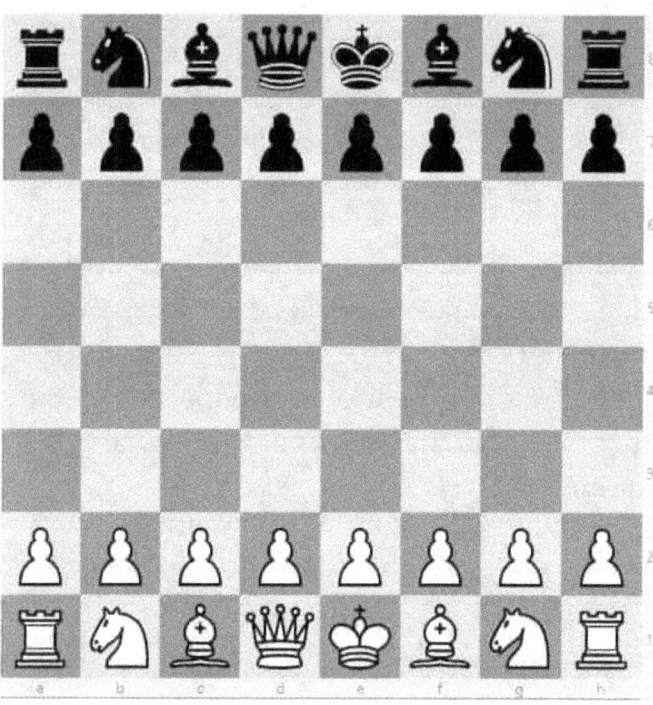

It is all quite easy

Even if you cannot play like a grandmaster yet, you can always do whatever you can to be a professional before the game begins. You can learn how to fill out the score sheet and learn chess etiquette – before the game begins, you can make some friendly chitchat and wish your opponent luck with a firm, sincere handshake. However, if you do not know how the right chess pieces set up, it will automatically flag you as a beginner (or a patzer, in chess parlance).

Learning proper chess pieces set up, and setting the right chess board can look complicated at first, but after a little practice, you will get the hang of it. You could also land the battle's first psychological blow if your opponent set their side of the board incorrectly – nothing would make you feel so smug as to point out that your opponent put their queen on the wrong square before the game even began.

Do a final review of the pieces and their positions before starting the game to ensure the chess board set up was done correctly.

- Are all the squares on the first and second row occupied?
- Have you used all the pieces in the chess set?
- Do all the pieces mirror each other? (For example, the white king should directly face the black king on the other side of the board)
- Is the bottom-right square (from either player's perspective) a light square? If not, you will have to go back to step 1 and start again.

When all chess pieces are set up the real game starts. White pieces player always goes first. If you are playing in a friendly game, you can determine who is playing white and who is playing black by shooting a coin, hiding a pawn of each color behind your back and getting your opponent to pick, or just agree. When you have learned how to set up chess pieces, you can dive into the chess world and start playing your first games. There is no fear. All these laws are not as complex as you would think. Remember the chess rules easily with a little preparation.

BEST CHESS STRATEGY

Now you can set up a chess board! Maybe all this information was daunting, and you think it is a lot to recall now. However do not worry! After setting up the chess board a few times, it will feel normal and no longer pose a problem. Are you a chess beginner? Do you want to increase your odds of winning training games? Or in tournaments? Here is the best chess strategy tips for beginners. We will help you understand simple chess strategies.

Control the center from the opening to the end.

This is one of the most critical tips for beginners to learn. The center is the most important section of the board, since the pieces will have access to the entire board while they are right in the center. That is why this strategic theory is so important, and the world's best players have proven it over and over. These players often try to keep their pieces pressing the middle.

Develop all your pieces as quickly as possible

It is also really important to build your pieces quickly. As your pieces are like your army, they are the ones that will help you conquer the board and ultimately help you win the games. Fast not designing the pieces can be a serious mistake. By not creating your pieces quickly, you could give your opponents more room on the board. You could swap off the board easily.

Do not move the same piece multiple times in the opening.

Not moving the same piece several times in the opening goes along with quickly improving the pieces. This is because multiple moving the same piece helps your opponent to develop more pieces much faster. There are moments you need to move the same piece several times to prevent losing the piece or anything else. However, this idea must always be kept in mind.

Protect your king by castling as soon as possible.

One of the key chess strategies is to always keep your king secure when trying to build vulnerabilities around your opponent's king if possible. That is why you should castle your king as soon as possible. It moves away from the center, which is the board position where most of the activity normally occurs. It also helps faster get your rooks to the middle.

Do not move your queen too early.

Not moving the queen too early in the game is one of the chess strategy tips for beginners. Most beginners attempt to move the queen too early to establish f7 or f2 mating threats. Typically these threats are not actual, and the player moving the queen usually loses some tempos trying to get the queen back to a safe square. You have seen this many times before. But "do not move your queen too early in the game" is a rule often omitted. For example, if your opponent makes a big mistake that you can punish immediately by beginning a queen attack.

Activate your rooks

The rooks are the hardest pieces to activate. They can only move horizontally and vertically. Without open columns, moving these heavy pieces is not easy. That is why caslting your king early is very necessary. It helps move one rook closer to the middle. You should also always try to predict which columns are most likely to be opened throughout the game, so you are the first to take advantage of open columns with your own rooks.

Think twice before moving your pawns.

As you know, pawns can only move forward. That is why it is a fundamental chess technique for all-level players, not just beginners. Another really important chess strategy tip is that pawns are the pieces with more mobility limitations. So pawns are often very necessary to decide the position's existence and the plans each player should pursue.

Eradicate a bad piece quickly

Identifying that any single piece has no promising future is a very critical element of chess strategy at all levels. This essentially separates inexperienced players from masters. When a bishop is blocked by his own pawns because they are in the same color as the bishop's squares, the bishop is generally considered a bad piece. It is prudent to replace it with another piece with the same value if possible.

Bishops tend to be stronger than knights are when they are wide open. Knights tend to be stronger pieces in closed positions, since they are the only pieces that can leap over other pieces.

Many beginner chess players feel frustrating during their first chess games. They easily fit. Or lose control of roles without knowing what happened. Or with several extra pieces, stalemate their rivals, throwing away a victory for a draw. Each chess player remembers the days when he or she tries to capture as many pieces as possible without any significant clue as to how to check the opponent with all the extra pieces. These circumstances can be quite discouraging, particularly for children starting a chess career. Following the above chess strategy tips will help you stop them.

Pawn structure and position

It is not a secret that the pawns help you win games. Beginners often underestimate their strength, but that is a big mistake. Strong pawn arrangement typically implies a solid position.

How do you identify good pawns?

- Most of the pawns are interconnected.
- The pawns occupy and control the center.
- The pawns pressure your opponent's position.
- In your position, the pawn structure did not produce holes or weak squares.

Good pawn structure.

White's pawn structure is good here because almost all the pawns are connected, the king is secure, the center is very strong with the e5 and d4 pawns, and while the white squares that go from c2 to f5 are "weak," white's queen and bishop work together to avoid any problems.

Now let's see what a bad pawn structure looks like:

All white pawns on the queenside (left) and center are small, as no other pawns help them. Also blacks now dominates the middle. White pawns will start dropping one by one over the next few moves, and black will win.

Getting rid of bad pieces

A "bad piece does not contribute to the position. There are several explanations. For example, a piece can be "trapped" in your area.

The b1 knight is a bad piece here

This white knight on b1 has zero operation and no positional impact. It cannot go anywhere. That is why you should swap your bad piece as soon as possible.

Controlling the center

During the opening phases of any chess game, your pawns and pieces have one simple goal: dominate the center. There is nothing more important they can do. Seriously, that is. To learn the best chess strategy tips for beginners, this is a must. There are many ways to battle the pieces for the middle.

Few simple examples of good centers:

That is the absolute middle. White's pawns occupy all central squares and pieces back up the pawns.

White's center is also good here, as both its central pawns occupy important squares (d4 and e5). Black threatens the middle with the queen on b6, knight on c6 and pawn on c5, but white will hold on without major issues.

This center varies slightly from previous ones. Although white does not occupy the center with its central pawns, they still have control over the most important squares, sooner or later moving their pieces. This is a slower but secure approach to monitor the opening and middle game hub.

Ensuring the king is safe

Our king is the most important board piece. It should be covered at all costs. As the game starts, the board is full of pieces and plenty of openings for both sides to strike. That is why it is important to get your king safe once you have got the chance.

If you start chess and want to improve, castle early. It is easy.

Generally, you want to castle to the kingside (short castle). Like that:

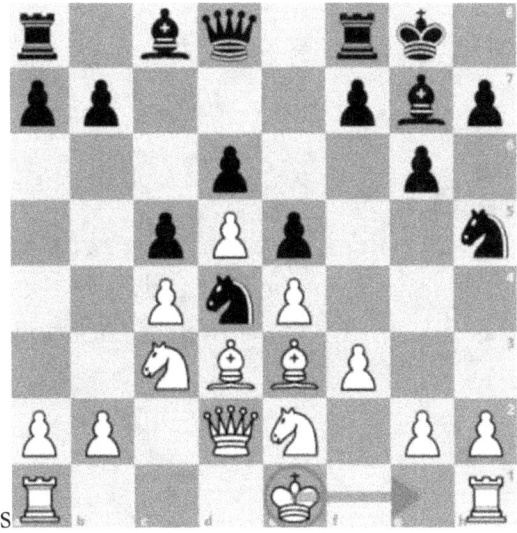

Short castle

If in that same position we would castle to the queenside (long castle)

Long Castle

Although our king will still be safer than he was in the center, this position gives black the chance to attack heavily on the queenside, advance the a- and b-pawns and carry the rest of their pieces.

Use your rook effectively

Rooks shine when there are few bits on the board. However in the game's opening and middle game phases, you can make the most of your rooks by following those simple guidelines. For example, if a file is open (this means no pawns in the way), one of your rooks should take care of that file where it can be most efficient.

The rook controls the open file

White rook sits on the e1 square where it dominates the entire e-file, placing additional pressure on black's position. Another smart idea is to position your rooks on the same files as your opponent's king and queen.

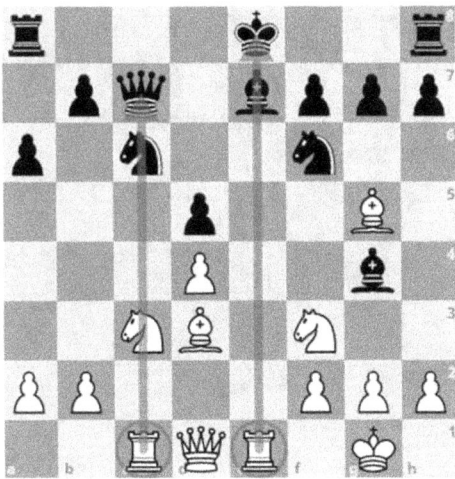

Rooks, indirect attack

By doing so, you strike both of the opponent's most valuable pieces indirectly.

Naughty queen

Our queen is our most important piece available. She is running like a rook, bishop, pawn and king. The queen is the most appropriate piece for launching killer attacks. Being such a strong piece, our queen is our opponent's clear target. We must be vigilant when we move it in the opening and middle game. We do not want our queen to be stuck, because that would mean we have lost the game.

Usually, you can move the queen very little in the game's opening process. When you find more room on the board, your queen will start doing her thing. Even if our queen is not stuck, we do not want to give the opponent the chance to quickly improve their pieces and gain tempo on our queen – we would have to move the queen multiple times to get it back to safety instead of bringing our other pieces into the game.

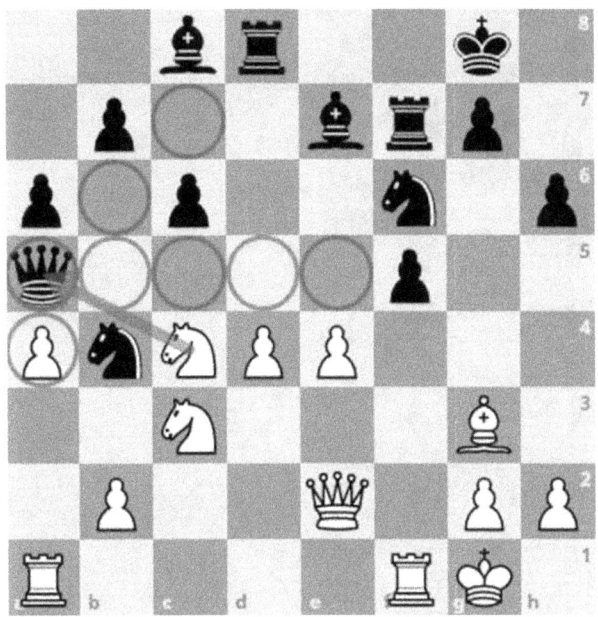

Trapped queen

Develop your piece quickly

You have certainly heard of this one. Create and develop the pieces quickly. This is one of the foundations of beginners' best chess strategy handbook. This means you should position your pieces on center-controlled squares and make it difficult for your opponent to create his pieces.

Good piece development

All the white squares have been completely made. The central pawns are solid, the king is secure, the rooks are connected. Perfect! On the other side of the board, black has only formed two pieces, the king is still in the middle, the rooks are still locked in on their starting squares, and the centre has very little battle.

Rest your pieces a little bit

While you should grow your pieces as soon as you get the chance, moving your pieces several times during the opening and middle game process is not advisable. The best thing to do is to move each piece once, build the rest of your pieces, and then move some of your pieces again. The reason is to complete your production as soon as possible, without delay.

Do not **waste time moving the same piece repeatedly.**

In the example above, black plans to move the knight several times, but none of the other pieces are created! What a time-waste. Stop these such futile maneuvers. Grow your pieces naturally and get closer to mastery. Why have the pieces on the board if you do not need them all?

If you are a chess novice, you can obey some general rules to progress. These 8 examples help you better understand chess and play more accurately. We have shown you the most popular positions you will find during a chess game. That does not mean you won't find several other common configurations, positions, and structures. Rest assured that these general rules and explanations will help you handle these situations effectively. Fight for the middle, grow your bits, and keep your king safe.

BEST CHESS OPENINGS

Your opening option is important for game progress. Openings are also very complex to beginners. Learning them correctly by heart can be incredibly difficult. So it would be wise to choose playing basic newcomer chess instead of cramming in those theoretical lines.

Not all openings fit beginners as well as experts. There is plenty of chess openings out there and you would need too much time to master them all. Playing too many openings is definitely not advisable. It is common that many beginners have more than one answer to some opening moves, but they know common plans and ideas in none of their chess openings. They respond to whatever their opponent does without their own "pet line".

These players never really control the game because their opponent gets the initiative and controls in which direction the game goes. A much safer solution is to continue to learn more and more information in the one that you enjoy, and to refrain from playing many different ones that you only have some shallow knowledge.

Many openings require intimate knowledge of deep, strategic ideas and subtleties of movement. First of all, remembering these 5 opening principles is key:

1. Control the center. (Specifically the e4, d4, e5, d5 squares)
2. Develop your pieces to actively create threats.
3. Try not to move a piece twice.
4. A knight on the rim is dim. (Developing towards the center greatly increases the mobility and scope of your pieces)
5. Get your king safe. (Leaving your king in the center can dangerously expose you to tactics)

One question that often occurs when evaluating a successful method of chess training is "what are the best chess openings for beginners to play?"

After all not all openings are as suitable for beginners as experts. Many openings require intimate knowledge of deep, strategic ideas and subtleties of movement. Copying your favorite players' chess openings is pointless if you do not grasp the underlying concepts. For beginners, there is no need to reinvent the opening wheel. Focusing on classic chess concepts like controlling center and creating pieces is much easier. This will do more for your chess than memorising an exact sequence of moves.

Ruy Lopez or Spanish Opening.

The Ruy Lopez has been one of the most common openings in chess for a long time, it starts with 1.e4 e5 2.Nf3 Nc6 3.Ab5. The key idea for white is to place pressure on the e5 pawn very early, white also develops the bishop in a good square and prepare to castle kingside.

The Ruy Lopez is possibly the key 1.e4 e5 chess opening in the game.

It starts with 1.e4 e5 2.Nf3 Nc6 3.Bb5.

One of the greatest chess players of all time, Vishy Anand, says if you are starting in chess or want to see real progress, you have to know how to play the Ruy Lopez. Because of its strategic nature and the fact that it leads to both open and closed positions, it is perfect for deepening general chess understanding.

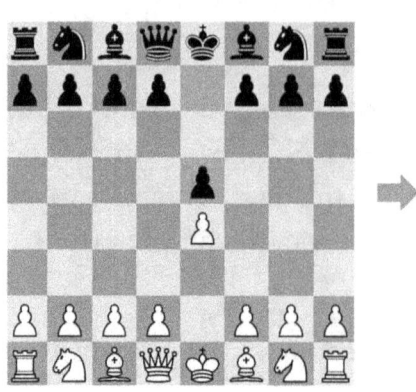

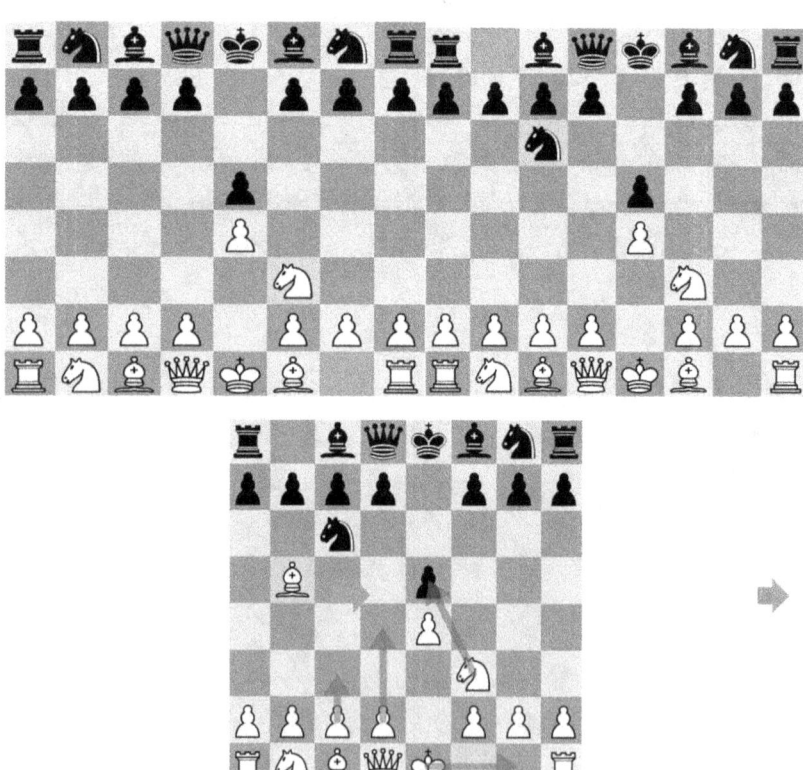

By Nazar1005 1.e4e52.Nf3Nc63.Bb5! The Ruy Lopez, the most popular opening in chess, white attacking e5 is his main idea of opening. White are developing the bishop on good position and prepare to castle kingside.

The Giuoco Piano or Italian Opening.

The Italian Opening or Giouco Piano is not only one of the oldest chess openings, but one of the most commonly played at all stages. It begins with the following moves: 1. 2.Nf3 Nc6 3.Bc4.

The Italian Game features moves 1.e4 e5 2.Nf3 Nc6 3.Bc4. White and black both occupy the middle and assist them with their knights. Then white develops the bishop to the square c4, and controls the diagonal a2-g8. But black is good here and has several moves at his disposal, including 3...Bc5, 3...Nf6, 3...Be7 and 3...d6.

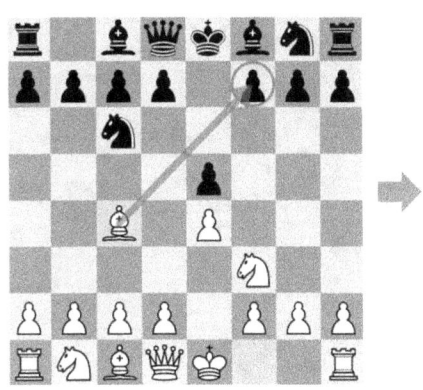

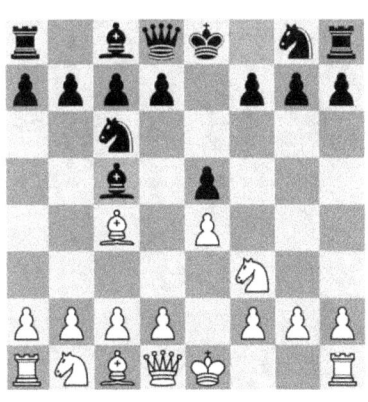 

1. e4e5 2. Nf3 Nc6 3. Bc4 This is the starting position of the Italian Opening. Here, black has two main moves at his disposal - 3...Nf6 and 3...Bc5.Bc53...Nf6 this move is playable for black, too. However, it allows white an aggressive extra option - 4.Ng5! 4.Ng5. If black knows what to do here, he does not need to fear this line. If he does not, however, he is already in huge trouble. White threatens to take on f7.4...d5 a strong move - blocking the diagonal for white's bishop. However, black temporarily sacrifices a pawn. 5. exd5. Black's main move here is 5...Na5 and the position becomes very sharp. We won't go into any detail here. However, it is important to note that black should only play the move 3...Nf6 if he knows how to play against 4.Ng5! 4.O-O white brings his king to safety. 4...Nf6 black develops his knight and wants to castle on the next move. 5.d3 white protects the e4-pawn .5...O-O 6. c3d6. Both sides castled and developed some of their pieces.

One of this opening's main ideas is to quickly monitor the middle. This is accomplished by putting a pawn in the center on the first move (1.e4), which also activates the light-squared bishop and white queen. By playing 2.Nf3, white immediately attacks e5's black central pawn. White moves his bishop to the risky c4 square (3.Bc4) from where he sees black's potentially vulnerable f7 pawn. Moreover by playing the bishop, white prepares to castle on the next move.

Following these concepts, white achieves the 3 key goals of any opening: centre power, rapid progress, and safety casting planning. White will continue castling, playing his knight to c3, the d-pawn to d3, and then taking the dark-squared bishop into play.

The Four Knights Opening

The Four Knights Opening is a fairly popular chess opening among beginners who adhere to the principle "develop knights before bishops". The Four Knights Opening usually leads to quiet positional play although there are some fairly sharp variations. The games usually start with the moves 1.e4 e5 2.Nf3 Nc6 3.Nc3 Nf6, after these moves white usually develops the bishop with 4.Bb5 and blacks does the same with 4... Bb4.

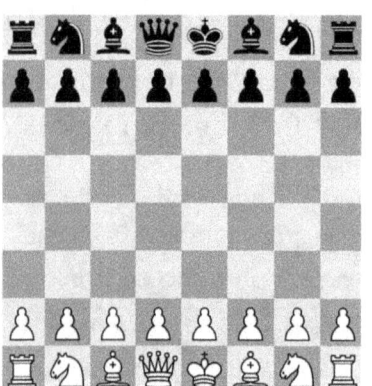 

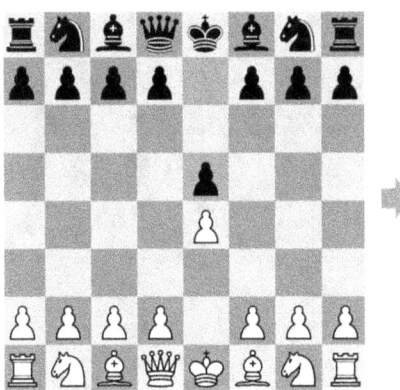

The Two Knights Defense or "Fried Liver".

This place comes to the board after moving 1.e4 e5 2.Nf3 Nc6, this is a very common moving order in games beginning with 1.e4, from here we might hit the opening Ruy Lopez or even the Giouco Piano. After 3.Bc4 Nf6 moves, the Two Knights' Defense's key position was reached. This defence is complex for black, where several variations result in a pawn's loss for more activity.

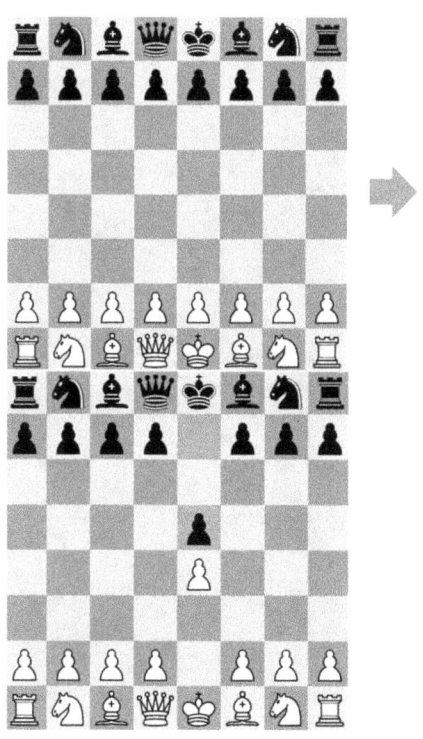
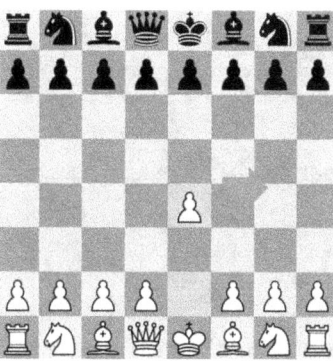

Queen's Gambit Accepted

The Queen's Gambit Accepted is a very old opening, as old as chess writing. Definitely one of the best openings for beginners who want to challenge the experience of white in this style of openings and try to win with black pieces. Many inexperienced players, after temporarily sacrificing a pawn, simply play the Queen's Gambit without really understanding how to implement strategies that give white an active play. This opening, first described by chess writers in the 15th century, became a feature in the 1886 Steinitz-Zukertort match. Black here embraces white gambit pawn. However, as we will see, black won't be able to retain this extra pawn.

It looks like white gives away the c-pawn, but black cannot hold on to the extra pawn for long. By playing c4, white will swap c-pawn (a flank pawn) for black's d-pawn (a center pawn). By capturing white's c-pawn immediately, we get rid of the burden, and now white must determine how to continue the game. Accepting white's sacrifice with dxc4 is totally fine and afterwards it is not necessary to try to defend the pawn. It is easier to keep creating parts and press the middle.

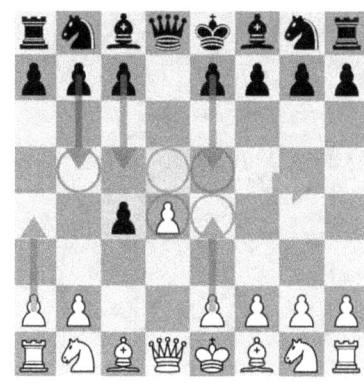

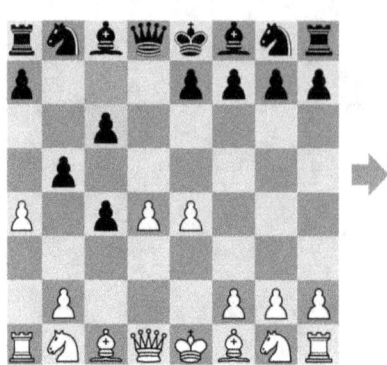

100

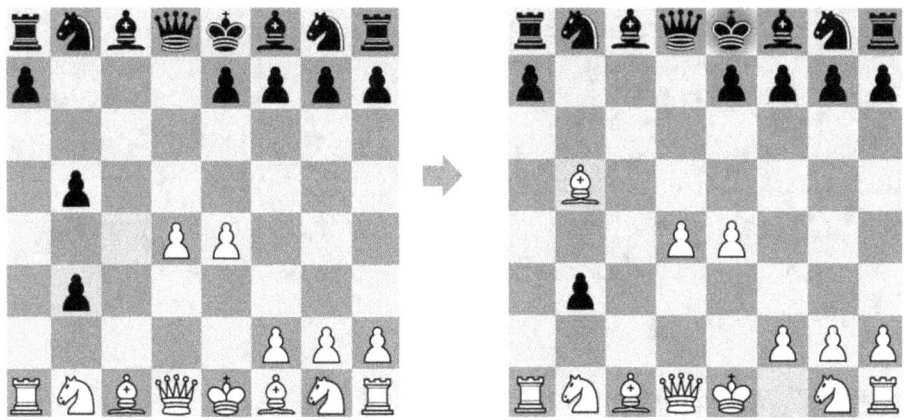

The QGA is an opening as old as chess writing. It was first mentioned in the 15th century by chess writers and became a feature in the Steinitz-Zukertort match of 1886. Here black accepts the gambitted pawn by white. However, as we will see, black will be unable to hold onto this extra pawn. Furthermore by capturing away from the center, this gives white free control of the center. It is argued however, that black will later play for some positional pluses by arguing that later in the game he can force an IQP (Isolated Queen Pawn) for white. Although the IQP gives chances for both players, in the endgame this positional weakness can turn out to be problematic for white as it becomes increasingly difficult to defend.

Furthermore, capturing away from the center gives white free use of the center room. It is argued that black would later play for certain positional pluses by producing an isolated white pawn. While this isolated pawn gives both players chances, this positional weakness can be problematic for white as it becomes increasingly difficult to defend.

The Queen's Gambit Declined

The Queen's Gambit Declined (or QGD) is a chess opening where black declines a white pawn in Queen's Gambit. This is known as Gambit Decline's Orthodox Line. When mentioning the "Queen's Gambit Declined," connection is generally presumed to the Orthodox Line.

Playing 2...e6 unlocks black's dark-squared bishop thus obstructing his bishop's light-square. By declining white's temporary pawn sacrifice, black erects a stable position; d5 and e6 pawns give black a foothold in the middle.

The Queen's Gambit Declined has a reputation as one of black's most reliable 1.d4 defences. In this case, white will try to manipulate black's light-squared bishop's passivity, and black will try to release it, trade it or prove the bishop's useful defensive position while passive.

An eventual ...dxc4 by black will yield the centre to white, and normally black won't do this unless he can obtain a concession, usually in the form of gaining a tempo, by capturing on c4 only after white first played Bd3.

In the Orthodox Line, the tempo battle revolves around white's attempts to play all other useful moves before playing Bd3.

The London System

The London System is certainly considered one of the best chess openings for beginners who have no time to research several opening systems and want a solid opening to play with white, whatever black plays. This generally follows 1.d4 and 2.Bf4 or 2.Nf3 & 3.Bf4. It is an opening "system" that can be used against practically any black defence, and thus involves a smaller opening theory than many other openings.

The London System is one of the Queen's Pawn Game openings where white opens with 1.d4 but does not play the Queen's Gambit. It normally results in a closed game.

The Sicilian Defense.

Sicilian Defense is the most common defense against white opening 1.e4 and is commonly used in top-level play. It is a rather aggressive defense and instantly stakes claim in the middle, denying white the e4 and d4 double pawns.

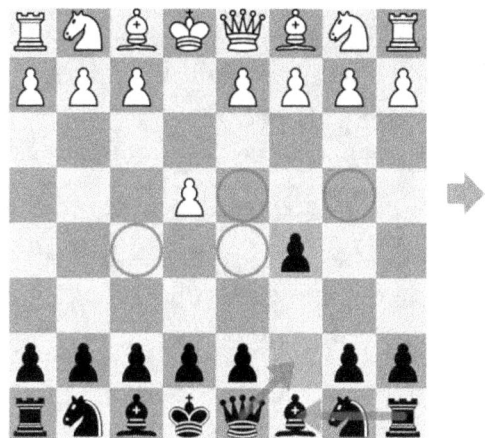

Many chess champions generally prefer 1.d4 because of how well the Sicilian Defense plays against 1.e4.

Typically, black's c-pawn is exchanged, opening the semi-open c file for black to carry his queen or rook and adding pressure to the queen side attack.

White has not only to think about black's defense, but also the counterattack posed by the Sicilian Defense. White appears to have the king side advantage while black typically looks to target the queen side.

Grandmaster John Nunn attributes the popularity of the Sicilian Defense to "its combative nature; in many lines black is playing not just for equality, but for the advantage. The drawback is that white often obtains an early initiative, so black has to take care not to fall victim to a quick attack". Grandmaster Jonathan Rowson considered why the Sicilian is the most successful response to 1.e4, even if Rowson wrote: There is a simple answer for me.

To take advantage of the initiative given by the first pass, white must take advantage of his opportunity to do something before black has equal opportunities of his own. To do this, however, he must 'contact' the black position. The first point of contact usually comes as a pawn exchange, which leads to place opening. ... So the thinking behind 1...c5 is this: "OK, I am going to let you open the position and build your pieces aggressively, but at a price – you have got to give me one of your pawns."

The Dutch/Stonewall Defense.

Stonewall Defense is an incredibly powerful black against 1. D4 – a sturdy structure very difficult for white to crack. Stonewall Defense includes putting black pawns on light squares d5, e6, and f5 to create an iron grip on the middle, explicitly limiting a possible breakthrough with an e4 drive.

Even if you are not crazy about playing the Stonewall Defense against any white set-up in the queen pawn opening systems, the Stonewall Defense is incredibly flexible and quick to transpose to black against 1. D4, 1. D4, 1. C4, 1. C4. Nf3, ect.

How to play and study chess openings?

- Do not play too many chess openings; become an expert in the few chess openings you prefer to play.
- Do not only memorize moves; understand your chess openings main ideas.
- Play according to the basic opening principles.
- Do not only study chess openings, but test them in real games, blitz games also help.
- The Italian Game, the Sicilian Defense, and the Queen's Gambit are some of the best chess openings for beginners to start with.

Other important moves

We recommend you start by mastering any of these:

- King's Indian Defense.
- Bogo-Indian Defense.
- Nimzo-Indian Defense.
- Queen's Indian Defense.
- Grunfeld Defense.

- **King's Indian Defense.**

It is a classic.

The King's Indian Defense follows 1.d4 Nf6 2.c4 g6 3.Nc3 Bg7. It is a common all-level opening option. To win as black against 1.d4, this is a tool you would do well to know. King's Indian Defense promises active black play.

Black will resist early simplifications and enter unbalanced positions, allowing him to play more than equality.

King's Indian Defense

- **Bogo-Indian Defense**

It is a good opening to surprise your opponent. 1.d4 Nf6 2.c4 e6 3.Nf3 Bb4+.

Black's idea is to postpone putting his pawns in the centre and quickly build the kingside instead. Bogo-Indian Defense is versatile, sound, and needs little theory learning.

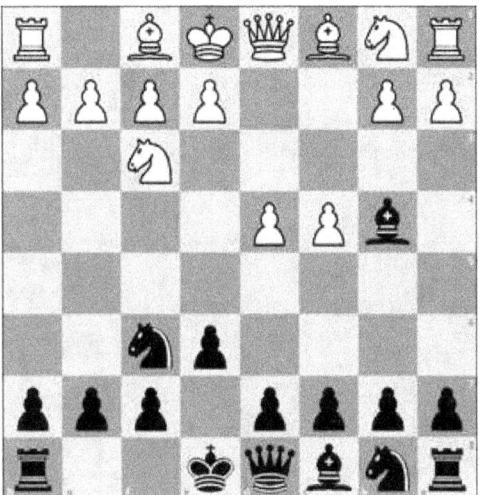

Bogo-Indian Defense

- **Nimzo-Indian Defense**

The Nimzo-Indian is similar to the Bogo-Indian except that black plays ...Bb4 while the white knight is already on c3. Starting with 1.d4 Nf6 2.c4 e6 3.Nc3 Bb4. The Nimzo-Indian Defense gives black chances of double-edged positions with rich resources to fight for victory.

Nimzo-Indian Defense

Queen's Indian Defense

The Queen's Indian Defense starts 1.d4 Nf6 2.c4 e6 3.Nf3 b6. Black can then fianchetto the bishop, place pressure on white's centre, or play the bishop on a6, and strike the c4 and e2 pawns. The Queen's Indian Defense is one of black's most versatile, dynamic ways to reach 1.d4.

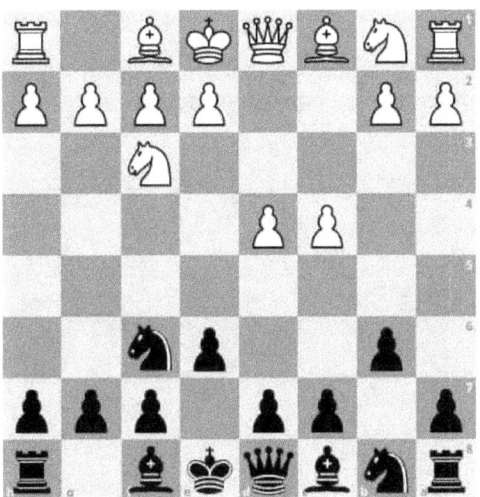

Queen's Indian Defense

- **Grunfeld Defense**

Many chess champions chose the Grunfeld Defense.

It starts with 1.d4 Nf6 2.c4 g6 3.Nc3 d5. Black does not try to dominate the center with his pawns early on but spends some time fianchettoing his dark-squared bishop and attacks the center with his pieces.

To put it into a simple formula: black leaves the center to white first then tries to conquer it because of its better growth.

Grunfeld Defense

THE QUEEN'S GAMBIT DECLINED.

The Queen's Gambit Declined is a chess opening after 1.d4 d5 2.c4 e6 and is one of the most common openings in chess. You cannot sidestep them. It is important to have a clear plan of what to do during the game's first few moves, especially if you are a beginner.

Knowing the openings you play not only helps you from falling for cheap opening traps, but also helps you to get a good midgame spot. That is the aim of the opening – not to win in 5 moves with a mad attack, but to get into the middle game from which you can work. Today, we want to look at one of these chess openings – the Queen's Gambit Declined. Most beginner chess openings, like Italian Game, Ruy Lopez, Four Knights Game and Two Knights Defense, all start with 1.e4.

However as you probably know, 1.e4 is not the only successful first move in chess. Another perfect opening move to familiarize yourself is 1.d4. Although you can believe there is not much difference between the two, they lead to very different opening mechanisms with entirely different strategies and ideas.

White occupies the middle with a pawn right from the word go with both moves. There is a significant difference between 1.e4 and 1.d4. The 1.e4 move frees white's light-squared bishop and queen.

In comparison, the 1.d4 move frees the dark-squared bishop and to some degree, the queen. Moreover after 1.e4, the king's pawn is not secured, while the queen's pawn stays defended after 1.d4. These complexities somewhat alter the opening strategy. Each move causes black to respond differently. Most beginner chess games start with 1.e4 e5 moves.

However after 1.d4, black cannot just play 1...e5. White could easily take the 2.dxe5 pawn, and black would be a pawn. Players argued that 1.e4 or 1.d4 is the better opening move, but it really comes down to the player's style. Both have their pros and cons and were seen at the pinnacle of the chess, repeatedly played by the greatest players and World Chess Champions throughout history.

The Queen's Gambit Declined is a classic answer to 1. D4, and played by almost all the great players on both sides of the board. It is one of the best chess openings for beginners. Let's gradually examine this opening. The Queen's Gambit continues as follows:

By moving 2.c4, white threatens to swap c-pawn (a flank pawn) for black's d-pawn (a center pawn). White also proposes a pawn sacrifice, moving his pawn to c4, as the c-pawn is vulnerable. Therefore the first opening moves are called Queen's Gambit. Black can capture pawn with 2...dxc4. This is not a real gambit, however as black cannot hold on the pawn.

White quickly takes it back with 2...dxc4 3.Qa4+, recapturing the pawn one move later) or playing 3.e3, threatening to catch c4 with the next move. Black must be careful not to hold the pawn desperately:

Instead of accepting the pawn sacrifice with 2...dxc4 (the Queen's Gambit accepted), black plays another logical move: 2...e6

That is what is called Queen's Gambit Declined mainline. Black refuses the "pawn sacrifice" and builds a stable position as black secures tight central control on e6 and d5.

CHESS TACTICS

"While tactics can sometimes be very complicated, there are good news: tactics consist of basic elements that can be learned as a language or mathematics." Many difficult chess tactics are a set of basic tactical elements. Therefore, if you want to solve complex chess puzzles, you need to know all the various basic forms of chess tactics. Therefore the following is dedicated to basic chess patterns and gives you an overview of 5 important tactical motifs.

A pin

A pin is a condition where a player's piece cannot or cannot be moved for these reasons:

- The king will be placed on check, as any move is illegal. It is an absolute pin;
- The opponent may catch a valuable piece. This is a relative pin as the move can be made, but it is typically not very successful.

In chess, there are three pieces that can pin other pieces. These are the three pieces: a rook, a queen, or a bishop. A pinning piece eye is one of the valuable pieces of the enemy, with a less valuable piece in its way. It is important to remember that relative pins can be risky on both sides, as your opponent can still move the pinned piece anyway. That is what both players forget.

In this position, black was playing 1...Qh7 with a check. At first sight, 1...Qh7+ looks like a 2.Rh3 error, but black has a great tactical resource in store. He plays 2...Rd1+, allowing white play 3.Kh2. Now black has the decisive blow 3...Rh1+! Four.Kxh1 Qxh3+! The pawn on g2 is pinned as the black bishop controls the diagonal a8-h1 (an absolute pin). White is forced to play 5.Kg1 and 5, Qxg2 is mate

This is a great illustration to explain why looking at the whole board in chess is always really important, not just the side of the board where the action takes place.

The next location shows the danger of pins on both sides. Looking at the location without measuring any row, white's position seems hopeless. His queen is pinned against the king, and no other piece can defend him. However, hold on a minute and do not hurry to resign! White is a little trick. He should play 1.b6!! + offering black's king two choices.

2.Rh8+ saves the day for white as black's only move to stop the check is 2...Qe8 and after 3.Rxe8+ Rxe8 4.Qxe8+ white mates the black king.

Black must take the pawn on b6 with his king – 1...Kxb6. white can use the fact that the black king is on the same rank as the rook and plays 2.Rh6! Black is losing! He cannot defend his rook, and he cannot take white's rook because the pin against his queen would lose material (2...Rxh6 3.Qxe7).

The fork

A fork is a move that simultaneously targets two or more enemy pieces. A fork's serious advantage is that it is hard to parry two threats with one move.

White's pieces appear much more successful in diagram position than black's army. White's queen is under assault, however, and if the queen retreats, white's move ...c7-c6 (attacking the knight on d5 defending the rook on e7) is quite unpleasant.

White wants a straightforward solution to his issues. 1.R1xe6! eliminates heavy black knight on e5 and forces black to swap 2...dxe5.

White follows up with 2.Rd7! attacking the black queen which has no as squares as 2...Qc8 loses to the fork 3.Ne7+ and 2...Qe8 loses to another fork – 3.Nf6+.

The Discovered Check

Discovered check is giving check by moving a piece that was blocking another of your pieces from giving it.

See for example, the following position:

Moving white is hanging the rook on b6. If he exchanges rooks on b1, turning his extra pawn into a long endgame struggle is not easy.

Fortunately, white has a more compelling option. He can begin playing 1.Ng6! Next pass is threatening mate on h8. Black has no alternative and must take the b6-1...Rxb6 rook. Now white can use a discovered check to win back his material investment and even catch a rook. 2.Nf8+ Kg8 (Kh8 won't change anything) 3.Nxd7+ 3...Kf7 4. Nxb6. Nxb6. White is a rook up quickly transforming its material advantage to a full point.

Promotion and under-promotion

If one of your pawns reaches the chessboard's 8th (or 1st) rank, you can "promote" it by turning it into another piece, normally a queen.

If you promote a pawn to a piece other than a queen (a knight, a bishop or a rook), then we call it "under promotion." Consider the following example:

White plays 1.Re8+ Rxe8, now 2.Qxg7+ Kxg7 3.fxe8=N+!

White does not promote his pawn into a new queen, leaving him with a lot of work to do before the game is over. However, he is promoting his pawn into a knight, forging king and queen. With this little trick, white's material advantage is decisive now.

Back-rank checkmate

The last strategy we will look at is the back-rank buddy. In this scenario, a rook or queen gives mate by going back to the chessboard's 1st or 8th rank, and the opponent's own pawns prevent the king from escaping. To explain this technique of chess, we will look at a famous example from the third world chess champion, José Raúl Capablanca.

5 Chess Styles – Definitive Tactics Guide

The diagram's position was reached after white's 29th move. White is a pawn up, but he faces serious back-rank problems, as his king has no square in the first rank.

He relies on queen and rook securing all the essential squares in 1st rank.

But Capablanca found a way to use circumstances and played the winning move 29...Qb2! Whatever white plays, he loses the game.

30.Qxb2 loses 30...Rd1, 30. After 30...Qb1+ 31.Qf1 Qxc2 and 30.Rc8!? (Perhaps better for white as black loses 30...Rxc8 due to 31.Qxb2) loses 30...Qa1+ 31.Qf1 Qxf1+ 32.Kxf1 Rxc8.

How to play the Queen's Gambit Declined

The Queen's Gambit Declined is a chess opening after 1.d4 d5 2.c4 e6 and is one of the most common openings in chess. Chess openings in any chess game. You cannot sidestep them.

It is important to have a clear plan of what to do during the game's first few moves, especially if you are a beginner. The opening process sets the base for the game's rest.

Knowing the openings you play not only helps you from falling for cheap opening traps, but also helps you get a good middle game spot. That is the aim of the opening – not to win in 5 moves with a mad attack, but to get into the middle game from which you can work.

However as you probably know, 1.e4 is not the only successful first move in chess. Another perfect opening move to familiarize yourself is 1.d4. Although you can believe there is not much difference between the two, they lead to very different opening mechanisms with entirely different strategies and ideas. White occupies the middle with a pawn right from the word go with both moves. There is a significant difference between 1.e4 and 1.d4. The 1.e4 move frees white's light-squared bishop and queen.

Players argued that 1.e4 or 1.d4 is the better opening move, but it really comes down to the player's style. Both have their pros and cons and were seen at the pinnacle of the chess, repeatedly played by the greatest players and World Chess Champions throughout history.

The Queen's Gambit Declined is a classic answer to 1. D4, and played by almost all the great players on both sides of the board. It is one of the best chess openings for beginners. Let's gradually examine this opening. The Queen's Gambit is as follows:

1.d4 d5 2. c4

By moving 2.c4, white threatens to swap c-pawn (a flank pawn) for black's d-pawn (a center pawn). White also proposes a pawn sacrifice, moving his pawn to c4, as the c-pawn is vulnerable.

Therefore the first opening moves are called Queen's Gambit. Black can capture pawn with 2...dxc4. This is not a real gambit, however as black cannot hold on the pawn. White quickly takes it back with 2...dxc4 3.Qa4+, recapturing the pawn one move later) or playing 3.e3, threatening to catch c4 with the next move. Black must be careful not to hold the pawn desperately:

Queen's Gambit Accepted moves

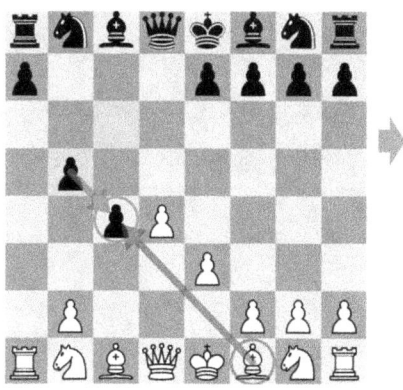

Instead of accepting the pawn sacrifice with 2...dxc4 (the Queen's Gambit Accepted), black plays another logical move:

2...e6

The Queen's Gambit Declined (QGD) starts with 1.d4 d5 2.c4 e6

That is what is called Queen's Gambit Declined mainline. Black refuses the "pawn sacrifice" and builds a stable position as black secures tight central control on e6 and d5.

Almost all black's pieces will become natural squares. Moreover the 2...e6 move frees the dark-squared bishop on f8 so that it can develop to e7, taking black one step closer to castling.

However the downside of 2...e6 is it currently blocks in black's light-squared bishop.

3.Nc3

Once white has a solid pawn core, it is time to build the minor pieces. 3.Nc3 is a rational option, since it fulfils several goals at once: it monitors e4 and d5 squares while preventing Bb4+.

White wants to play e2-e4 at some point, gaining even greater centre share. The knight on c3 supports this initiative.

3...Nf6 4. Bg5

Many beginners will immediately try to overcome the center pressure by exchanging pawns. For either side, this is not a smart idea. Black does not want c4 so white can play e4, making a right pawn center. White certainly won't take on d5 because after ...exd5 black finishes with both bishops open and ready for action.

Black exposes the knight of his king stopping white's attempt to advance e-pawn to e4. White responds by pinning the queen's knight, briefly immobilizing the knight. White is ready to play e4 on the next move, so black needs something different to avoid that.

4...Be7

Black unpins his f6 knight, builds the bishop, and prepares to castle. White could potentially swap his g5 bishop for knight and play e4, but that would only give black an advantage in terms of faster development and a bishop pair.

Plan for white

White plays e3 after bishop exchange. This is a very good move that sets up a solid c4-d4-e3 pawn chain, allowing a light-squared bishop and queen on the b1-h7 diagonal.

White gets ready for castle. His plans include relocating the rook to c1 and playing e4 at the right time, establishing a powerful central presence. This is a very good place for white to play, as he has a space advantage and with the e4 advance can get some action going in the middle.

Plan for black

Black develops slightly behind. However he has the bishop's advantage and can castle instantly. By comparison, black has a bishop problem on c8, blocked in by his own e6-pawn. Black must find out how to free it. One idea for black is a well-timed c5 attack.

The Queen's Gambit Declined is one of the best openings for beginners to try, particularly if for one reason they do not want to play e4 openings. It is playable for both colors and can lead to a sluggish, positional or sharp tactical game depending on the opening choices. It is always a good idea to go through grandmaster games with the opening you are researching. Keep in mind that the opening is one aspect of the game. To be competitive in chess, you need to grasp middle game positions, have strong endgame strategy, spot chess tactics and much more.

How to learn chess openings

Chess openings enjoy growing publicity nowadays. Many chess players focus solely on chess openings, almost ignoring the rest of the game. New chess books and chess DVDs are published in increasingly short intervals. There is plenty of details and plenty of advertisements why you should have this or that opening in your repertoire. As a result, most chess players face great difficulties navigating through this jungle of novelties, trendy lines, and recommendations by opening experts. Furthermore, powerful chess engines refute former main lines that are no longer playable.

Moreover, sitting behind the chess board in a tournament, several club players have opening issues. Either they cannot recall their files they saved on their machines, they are not sure what to play because their opponent deviated from the key theoretical suggestions, or they mixed combinations and ideas simply because they tried to remember too much.

Learning new chess openings

While it may sound trivial, one of the most difficult aspects of creating a chess opening repertoire is to find positions that suit you and that you enjoy playing. Take the time and make sure that you really want to play this chess opening before studying. It is a waste of time to make a fast decision on an opening that you want to play as the key weapon in your arsenal for years and then throw it overboard after 3 months due to some painful losses.

You will need to make sure the opening suits well with your playing style when selecting a new chess opening. You should probably stay away from playing the Sicilian Najdorf or the King Indian Defense and select chess openings like the Caro-Kann or the Nimzo-Indian that require less memorization of concrete lines if you are an intuitive chess player who makes decisions on the chess board more based on general and abstract principles rather than concrete calculation and memorization of razor-sharp lines.

What is more, you should also make sure that you have a lot of fun playing it when seeking a chess opening that suits you.

Of course, it is important to play good chess openings, but you do not need to play 1.e4 e5 with black only because the vast majority of chess games between the world's best chess players begins with 1...e5 after 1.e4.

Other sound chess openings, such as the Caro Kann, Sicilian Defense or the French, may also be played.

It will inspire you to work on your opening abilities and to learn theory if you enjoy playing the positions resulting from your opening.

Remember the best openings in chess are the ones you love playing!

Here are some short lists of chess openings for black against 1.e4 and 1.d4. The first two lists include openings for sound chess that you can play daily.

There are interesting but somewhat questionable openings in the final two lists that you can use only as surprise weapons and not as your main option against 1.e4 and 1.d4:

- **Best chess openings against 1.e4**: Ruy Lopez (Berlin Defense; Marshall Attack), Petroff Defense, Philidor Defense, Sicilian Defense (Najdorf Variation; Scheveningen Variation; Dragon Variation; Accelerated Dragon; Sveshnikov Variation; Kalashnikov Variation; Paulsen/Taimanov), French Defense, Caro-Kann Defense, Alekhine Defense, Pirc Defense

- **Best chess openings against 1.d4:** Queen's Gambit Declined, Tarrasch Defense, Slav Defense, Queen's Gambit Accepted, Gruenfeld Defense, King's Indian Defense, Nimzoindian Defense, Queen's Indian Defense, Bogo-Indian Defense, Dutch Defense (Stonewall, Leningrad Variation), Benoni, Benko Gambit.

- **Surprise openings against 1.e4:** Scandinavian Defense, Elephant Gambit

- **Surprise openings against 1.d4**: Albin Counter Gambit, Budapest Gambit, Chigorin Defense, Old Indian Defense.

Choose an opening and patiently practice

You should try to get an overview of the related material once you have selected an opening.

Starting with a chess book written for strong titled chess players is not recommended, which includes an endless amount of theory and just a small description of the fundamental concepts of your opening. Starting small is of extreme importance.

First, strive to comprehend the main concepts and recurrent themes of your chess opening. If you start studying the Sicilian Dragon, for example, if you have not been exposed to standard recurring patterns such as the trade sacrifice on c3, it makes little sense to learn long theoretical lines by heart in the Yugoslav Attack.

Learning to play a chess opening means learning to comprehend every move you make, not copying moves from databases, strong players or chess engines blindly.

How to become a chess opening expert

You need to devote a lot of time to carefully practicing your lines to become an authority on your chess openings. In just an hour or two, this process is not something you can get through. It is necessary, therefore, not to play too many openings in chess. Some chess players have more than one answer to some of the opening moves, but that means they are none of the experts! These players fear and overestimate the training of their opponent and move between their lines frequently.

That is superfluous! The simple, but remarkable phrase was said by Super-GM Peter Svidler: "I am more afraid of some players' opening preparation than others". Sure, if you play against opening specialists like Vladimir Kramnik or Anish Giri, you could get into trouble without adequate theoretical knowledge if you play a line that you always play.

As an ordinary club player, though, you do not usually get to compete with these top stars. If you play with an opposition rating of about 2000 Elo or less, you do not have to rack your brain against your opponent, refuting your favorite opening.

A much safer approach is to strive to become an expert in the one chess that you play, and to refrain from playing many different ones that you only have some superficial experience.

How to master your chess openings

You cannot become a chess opening expert on a new chess opening in one week. Of course, it is always a good idea to get an overview of all the variations that can emerge from the chess opening you play.

Do not only recall it but also write down all the variations. This helps you to keep track of your success. When you have done this you should start to explore each line a lot deeper. However, you cannot dive down both lines at the same time. It is a good idea to make a priority list of the lines you want to study.

Some variations occur at the chessboard more often than others. These are the lines you should approach first. You should assign yourself one or two weeks for each line – depending on the training time you spend on openings each week – and try to gain a deep understanding of what is going on in this variation. Always remember to archive your study in a database so that you can recheck it at a later stage. Only if you feel secure about the variation you studied, you can turn your attention to the next line.

As the human brain is naturally forgetful, however you need to repeat your opening lines from time to time. It takes time and effort, but it is necessary.

In each chess opening, there are many critical lines which you need to be prepared for. If you want to play very sharp lines, you need to know the theory—especially black. Check the vital lines, keep up-to-date, check the database's latest developments and pursue changes yourself.

Last but not least, measure the openings in real games. Gather experience playing with your opening while sitting on the chess board, thinking for yourself without chess books or chess engines.

Additional tips on learning chess openings

Work with another person: It may be a good friend, club mate, or chess coach. It greatly enriches your knowledge of opening chess if you have someone to chat about new ideas, vital lines, and planning for chess opening tournaments. You will analyze lines together and play on-the-spot training games against each other. The second person will also help you with your tournament openings.

Repair your lines: Do not lose faith in your variation from a crushing defeat. Fix your line, try again. Do not regularly turn openings. Become a chess opening specialist. It has many advantages. For example, your opponents cannot prepare you in blitz and rapid chess. Expertise beats versatility. Know the most popular chess opening traps in the lines you play. Knowing various opening traps helps you avoid being on the wrong side of a 10-move victory and allows you to win some fast games.

SECRETS OF THE MIDDLE GAME

Middle game is the most complex chess process, mixing tactics and strategy, attack and defense, pawn and piece play. So much happens that it can quickly become overwhelming. What is more, unlike the opening where you can memorize theory, the middle game is completely different! There are thousands of places you will find in.

In human games – as opposed to engines – it is extremely rare that the better-positioned player does not give his opponent any counter-chances. When reviewing strong-engine games, we can see how much we miss hidden tactical opportunities. You must be mindful of the possibility of discovering a tactical concept that can turn the game. Be alert and try to manipulate your opponent's errors.

Thankfully, british grandmaster Danny Gormally is here to demonstrate how to gain points and greatly improve your chess with dominant middle game play.

Unexpected tactical opportunities in the middle game

Danny analyses his own career game where such an opportunity emerged. The more you discuss these kinds of scenarios, the more often you can spot ways to turn around or stop making similar mistakes. Let's have a look. We start with the left place.

At this point, black played the move...Rc8, which turns out to be a serious mistake. A move like...e6 would have been easier.

Here we can examine the location. White's place looks promising. The knights are in the middle of the board, and the two bishops on c2 and d2 control nice diagonals. Place decent, centralized. A move like Qg4 now looks normal, threatening something like Nxg6 with some form of sacrificial attack. But we should also examine black's position here to see if we can find vulnerabilities!

Second, black does not have many kingside pieces to defend the king. Second, black's kingside pawns were weakened by pushing hand g pawns one square forward. This gives an impression that white should play in this position: Ng4. This move immediately attacks the pawn on h6, threatening it with a check. Black now has a difficult call about what to do.

The first alternative is...g5 but obviously not desirable. It produces even more position vulnerabilities, and white will move the knight around it, holding the pressure on. A move like...h5 is also problematic for Nh6+. Here in the right place, black does not really want to catch h6 as he loses the bishop.

In games where the bishop fianchettoed before a castled king, holding the piece on the board is key. In many cases, white can create an irresistible attack once the bishop defender is removed. Or as Bronstein said, "g7 mate" will follow.

Important middle game principle

Centralize your pieces

It is a well-known fact that far more squares power in the centerpieces than elsewhere. This is a particularly important rule when dealing with knights. When centralized, knights can control as many as 8 squares, while when cornered, just 2 squares. Real, bishops can be very successful from the flank. In the middle, however they are more mobile and monitor both board pieces. The same applies to the queen. If secure, bishops and queen and knights should be centralized.

Trade your flank pawns for the central pawns

Generally, central pawns are more valuable than flank pawns. This is because central pawns allow controlling important central squares (d4-d5-e4-e5) that can be used to support pieces and establish a strong attack not only in the center, but also on the side of the king or queen. Simultaneously, central pawns provide space and increase mobility. It is also advised not to exchange the central pawns for the opponent's flank pawns. You can simply do the reverse and exchange your flank pawns for the opponent's central pawns.

Avoid pawn weaknesses

A pawn vulnerability is something that can offer an immediate advantage to your opponent by manipulating them. That is something that can turn an identical endgame into defeat. To prevent endgame difficulty, take care of the pawn structure right from the opening and middle game. Stop duplicated, backward, disconnected pawns. Both white and black have significant pawn vulnerabilities underneath. White has doubled pawns, whilst black has isolated pawns.

Avoid creating weak squares in your position

A vulnerable square is a square unprotected by a pawn. Weak squares are ideal candidates for being solid outposts for the pieces of your enemy. The closest the weak square is to the location or middle of your king, the more trouble it typically causes. Always be vigilant with pawn advances, as this produces the vulnerable squares. Pawns cannot return.

In the diagram below white has a weak f3 square next to the location of his king. Black knight and queen will use it soon to establish mating threats.

Blockade your opponent's isolated pawn with a knight

An isolated pawn is a powerful weapon that your opponent can use to launch a strong attack since it supports pieces, providing extra space. Another threat is that isolated pawn can be moved forward at the right time, creating several problems. That is why blocking the opponent's isolated pawn to prevent complications is very necessary. The best piece for this reason is the knight.

Occupy open files with your rooks

It is no wonder rooks work best on open files. If an open file is available, your instinctual move should be to occupy the rook file. Next move is to double your open file rooks. If no open files are available, you can occupy a semi-open file that you can open later.

The position below white has a serious positional advantage since it controls the open file – the position's key element.

Keep the bishop pair

The bishop pair is strong in most positions. Only if the two knights are completely locked up they will be stronger than a bishop pair. Avoid giving up a bishop in the opening or early middle game just to build doubled pawns in the pawn structure of your opponent. In most cases, the bishop pair is targeting possible overweight pawn structure defects. Because of the bishop pair's ownership, the position below white has a serious positional advantage.

Bad chess opening moves

One of the worst first moves for white to play is 1.g4. With this move, white does not fight for the middle – an important principle in chess – and gives black a simple aim to strike. If black responds to 1.g4 with 1...d5! he occupies the centre and directly attacks white's loose pawn on g4 with his bishop on c8.

If white, for example, defends his pawn with a move like 2.f3, this can lead to a quick mate. The move 2...e6 looks harmless but threatens a deadly checkmate on h4 with the queen.

White can defend by playing 3.h4, but with 3...Bd6 black renews the threat of mating white on the e1-h4 diagonal. The move 4.Rh3 (defending against ...Bg3++) results in a beautiful mate in two. Black can sacrifice his queen with ...Qxh4 and after white takes the queen with 5.Rxh4 (there is no alternative), black ends the game with 5...Bg3++.

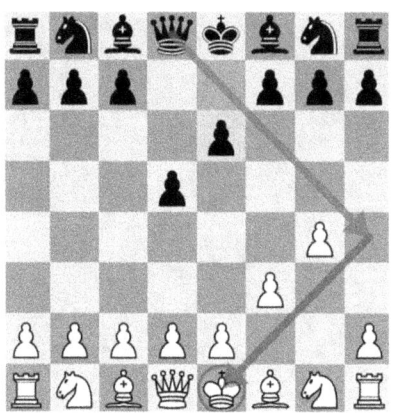

Admittedly, this example may be an unusual occurrence in practice, but it shows that black can take advantage of these bad opening moves by playing the simplest response moves.

Another poor opening move is 1.f3 as it irrevocably weakens the king position of white without doing anything useful. Bad moves include 1.Na3 and 1.Nh3. These chess movements neglect two fundamental rules at the same time – not only that a knight on the rim is dim," but they also compel white to move the same piece a second time in the opening, losing valuable tempo after black plays 1...e5 or 1...d5 by catching the knight with his bishop.

Dubious chess opening moves

1.H4, for example, is questionable. The move is not as bad as 1.g4, but it does not help gain control over the central squares. Furthermore, casting kingside is less desirable after transferring h4 as the kingside is weakened. Thus, extreme chess players seldom see the pass. Obviously, with this move, white cannot compete for an advantage, but it should not be too bad, as it causes no weaknesses.

Chess moves like 1.e3, 1.d3 or 1.c3 are playable and do not weaken white's position, but there is no point in playing them except to stop theory and brace the opponent. However since we are looking at all the moves from a beginner's viewpoint, we do not have to fear preparation at any amateur stage. Thus such chess moves waste time, interferes with developing all the pieces into useful squares, and they do not fight for control over the center.

1.g3, for example, is not a bad move and can translate into other openings such as English. However the main downside to this move is that black will occupy the center with any moves they wish to play. Essentially, it is recommended that every beginner avoid the before mentioned weird chess opening moves right from the beginning of their training as they can lead to rapid losses and disadvantageous positions from the very beginning.

Strong chess opening moves

As we saw, unless white occupies the center with their pawns, black has the ability to do so! Therefore, white plays active, space-gaining chess right from the start.

White can start by moving the queen's pawn to "d4," leading to openings like Queen's Gambit, King's Indian Defense, Nimzo-Indian, Bogo-Indian, Queen's Indian Defense, and Dutch Defense. Step 1.d4 has several strengths. It not only leads to controlling the center immediately, but also releases two pieces on the back rank with only one move.

1.E4 is chess' most famous opening move. One of the main ideas of this move is to quickly dominate the center with the pawn put in the center by the first move, releasing white's light-squared bishop as well as white queen. White can play Nf3 and move his bishop to the dangerous c4 square. From there, black's theoretically vulnerable pawn is on f7. By playing the bishop, white prepares to castle the next move.

Finally, it should be remembered that 1.c4 (English Opening) and 1.Nf3 (Reti Opening) are both good chess opening moves, leading to white solid and sound chess openings. Following these ideas, white achieves 3 main goals of any opening: center control, quickly create parts, and prepare to cast the king into safety.

The fundamental concepts discussed are here to help any beginner to develop their chess game and start their games with a suitable opening. If you keep these tactics at the forefront of your mind and refresh and deepen your skills from time to time, nothing can stand in your chess way. Do not forget the fundamentals of chess openings: battle for the center right from the start as white (if not the best you can get out of your opening is an equal position), do not give up your first mover advantage – (play actively), 1.e4 or 1.d4 are decent opening moves!

CHESS ENDGAMES

Chess endgames are the game's key component. To get more wins, it is important for all aspiring players to have a strong endgame plan for chess. Too many club players in the endgame go wrong and blame their loss on a move they played in opening.

At first, chess endgames can seem intimidating and overwhelming. Unlike the opening, moves cannot be memorized because every game you get will have different endgame positions. Some decisions are irreversible in chess. For example, piece exchanges cannot be retrieved. That is why you have to think twice about which endgame pieces to swap.

Due to the reduced endgame stuff, exchanging the right pieces is much more critical than in middle games. The endgame exchange decision should never be taken lightly. Often analyze carefully a potential move to a certain form of endgame. In fact, these main decisions on whether or not to trade is what distinguishes average players from big players.

However, decent endgame skills are crucial to any aspiring player. They will allow you to easily win seemingly equal positions with only small imbalances, save half a point from obviously worse positions, and avoid stalemate or draw-offs. And if you have all been marginally worse, you can turn the tables and win the game with superior endgame strategy. And because most club-level players do not spend enough time practicing the endgame, you are in a good place to really put the pressure on just like Magnus Carlsen's World Champ in his games. He is famous for grinding his rivals, progressively in the endgame, exhausting the opponent, and generally finding at least a half-point.

Chess endgames: transition

After an exchange of pieces, re-evaluate the position. Stay objective when determining position. For example, if you continually overestimate your role, things will end terribly. The location in the right diagram is a clear example of how challenging it can be to swap endgame pieces. Queens' exchange is more complex than any other pair of bits. Strong grandmasters, who struggle to make the right choice in these circumstances, may find several examples. In these crucial positions, you need to carefully analyze the resulting position after the queen's exchange to prevent a bad endgame. If you have enough clock time, your decision should not hurry. In the diagram on the right (from above, Smith – Lenderman), black offered a queen swap with 1...Qf7.

But it is a critical error as black's pawn endgame is lost. 2.Qxf7+ Kxf7 3.Kf3! (3.dxe6? e5!-+ and the black king picks up the white D-Pawn), white will win this endgame. See the left diagram. When you go for an exchange of pieces, it is also key to note small details in the place. These complexities play a tremendous endgame role.

For example, in the above position, the white a-pawn is still on a2 and not a3.

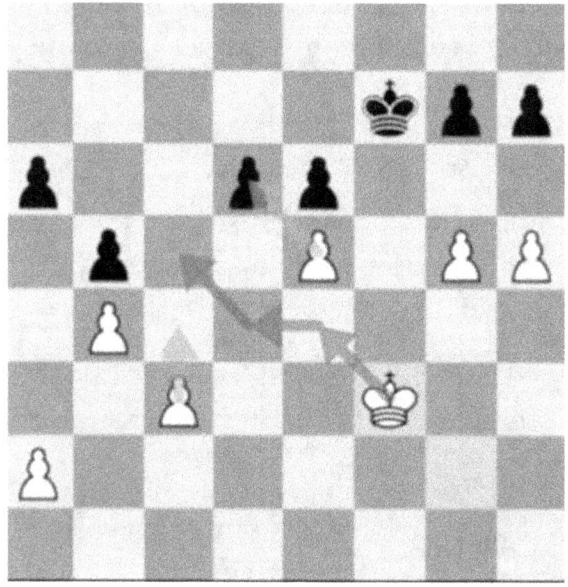

Isolated pawns – chess endgame strategy

The isolated queen's pawn is a common subject in chess, as it is a commonly seen pawn structure that can emerge from several different openings, beginning with 1. E4, 1. E4, 1. D4 or 1. C4. C4. One should know at least how to manage these isolated pawn systems.

By studying the grandmasters' games, GM Kuljasevic discusses how you should handle these positions in your own games and the general concepts you should adhere to. For example, if your opponent has an isolated pawn, try to take control of the square immediately in front of the pawn.

Another idea you can apply in games is trying to swap bits. If the opponent has an isolated pawn, they will want their pieces on the board. The less pieces they have the harder it will be to defend their position's vulnerabilities, giving you a target for your attacks.

Isolated pawns in the endgame

Davorin focuses particularly on the endgame's isolated queen's pawn and teaches you how to combat it. Sometimes, your opponent's isolated queen's pawn may become vulnerable.

You will need to know how to manipulate it and you will possibly need to look to establish a secondary weakness in the opponent's position.

Let's look at one of Davorin's video games analyses. It is a game with a Semi-Slav opening that skips through the middle game to go almost directly from the opening into the endgame. It began with 1. d4 d5 2. C4 c6-33. Nf3 Nf6 4. Nc3 e6 5. e3 Nbd7 6. Qc2 a6, reaching the position on the left.

Black's main move at this point is usually 6…Bd6. 6…a6 is a much rarer option, but it is still a practicable choice. After 7. b3 Bd6 8. Bb2 0-0 9. Bd3 e5, black looks to gain space in the centre. Playing …a6, white has no choice to play Nb5.

White 10-captures. Cxd5 11cxd5. Dxe512 Nxe5. Nxe5 Bxe5 and on the right, a position with an isolated pawn. The isolated pawn side should try to hold pieces on the board. If white were to castle now we would reach a middle game where black would play with the bishops on the kingside. This brings us our first chess strategy—attempting to swap pieces. White has played 13. Ne2. Ne2. This looks not only to swap the powerful bishop on e5, but this move also takes care of the square immediately in front of the isolated pawn – another idea to apply in these circumstances.

General chess endgame principles

Many club players spend very little time studying endgames. They are not familiar with critical theoretical endgames, nor concentrate on developing good understanding and technique of endgames. However, decent endgame skills are crucial to any aspiring player. You can easily win seemingly similar positions with only a little imbalance or save half a point from obviously bad positions.

Second, judging endgames correctly is a crucial skill. After an endgame piece exchange, you must re-evaluate the position. Stay objective in determining position. For example, if you continually overestimate your role, things will end terribly. Chess endgames rules vary fundamentally from middle games and openings. Therefore you need clear parameters to determine endgame positions.

In any endgame, the principle of piece operation is extremely significant. Try to set the pieces aggressively to avoid passive positions. Even at the expense of some content, this can significantly boost your role and help you win games that might not have at first appeared winnable.

Material is often less important than endgames initiative. It is important to understand: when comparing your pieces with the pieces of your opponent, you must not only determine which piece is currently better positioned, but also which piece has more potential. You must also determine the kings' position. King's centralization is one of chess endgame play's core rules. Generally speaking, the king's shifting position is one of the most important features distinguishing endgames from middle games and openings.

In the middle game, we have the king's defensive attitude. However in the endgame, an aggressive king can defend vulnerabilities, control important squares, and target vulnerable pawns so that more powerful pieces like rooks can be more effectively positioned and have no defensive tasks to fulfil. In the endgame, the king is generally considered to be worth 4 points.

Pawn structures play a key endgame role. Compare your pawn structure with your opponent's pawn structure. Has your opponent poor pawns or squares? Identifying vulnerabilities dictates your plan. If your opponent already has no vulnerabilities, try to build any.

White has an advantage here. His rooks are marginally better positioned, and b2's dark-squared bishop is better than e7's counterpart. Black's pawn structure is worse. The pawn on f5 can become a target, but squares e6 and g6 behind the pawn are weakened too.

It is also necessary to still look at the board as you regroup and strengthen your pieces. Emphasis not just on the board area where activity takes place. See the right place. In this place, black intended to mate white's king on the kingside. With white's king on h2 and black bishop still on d4, bringing the rook to the h-file was a serious threat.

White managed to knock black's bishop off d4, however and took his king to g1. Now, black should abandon his intentions to mate white's king on the kingside and move plans using the entire board. Not only can the f8 rook be carried to h8, but also moved to the queenside a8-square. The rook will go to second rank from there. 1...Ra8—white has no protection against the strategy.

Stalemate in chess

Stalemate is a special form of draw. It happens in a situation where the moving player has no legal move, but is not in check. Stalemate finishes with a draw, according to chess rules. Stalemate is a normal resource in the endgame. The player who defends a worse position will often by giving away stuff, try to seek a stalemate in such positions so as not to lose the game. The rule can seem counterintuitive at first glance. Why should a tie end if you deprive the opponent of some legitimate move? Should not it end in a crushing side victory? There has already been many discussions on this topic. However the existing chess rules describe stalemate as a draw, and this rule is unlikely to change anytime soon.

One side, when you are defending a hopeless position, we want to introduce you to stagnate as an effective defensive resource. On the other side, if you have a clearly stronger position, we also want to sharpen your eye for your opponent's stalemate ideas.

To understand the main stalemate concept, let's look at a simple example:

Stalemate is common in pawn endings. Moving in the diagram above is black, but the black king has no legal square to move. Since the black king is not in check, we have got a board stalemate. The game ends in drawing. We want to show you some simple stalemate patterns that every chess player should know.

Stalemate in beginner chess games

Stalemate occurs frequently in beginner chess, particularly in scholastic chess. Players know chess basic rules, but they have a vague understanding of how to match the opponent in such cases. Another example is a classic:

Objectively speaking, this position is white-winning. He has a whole queen, and black has just one king. Currently, many beginner players are unfamiliar with winning match trends. Instead of getting the king closer to the enemy's king to help the queen offer checkmate, they remove even more squares from the opponent's king. In the diagram above the 1.Qc7 movement appears at first glance as it traps the black king in the corner. However the problem with this move is that the king is not in check and cannot make moves. As black has no other pieces to move on the board, it is a stalemate. White could simply match black in two movements, beginning with 1.Kc6! Kb8 (black's legal move) 2.Qb7#.

Stalemate in chess endgames

Stalemate is the most possible endgame. On one hand, it may occur as a secret resource for the losing player to save a half-point. For several theoretical endgames, however, stalemate concepts are of great importance:

The endgame of king + bishop pawn vs a queen which is not supported by its king is a draw:

It is necessary to remember that the weaker side can use the same defensive resource to defend endgame king and rook pawn vs. a queen not protected by their king:

White's king is in charge. White does not need to play 1.Kf8, though? To give up h-pawn. He can go 1.Kh8! Now, black has no time to move his king closer as 1...Kc2 would be stalemate.

Stalemate is also a significant resource in dynamic theoretical endgames. Consider the endgame rook + bishop vs rook. Theoretically, this material mixture is a draw. In practice, however even powerful grandmasters sometimes cannot save the game. There are two key defensive setups in this endgame – Cochrane place and second rank defense. Knowing the latter is vital for tournament players:

Studying theoretical endgames cannot be overlooked. If you are familiar with the most important theoretical endgames and know which positions draw or win, you can actively target them in your games, whether you are attacking or defending. If you defend a worse position and know that the endgame rook + bishop vs rook is a draw due to the second rank defense, you can try to aggressively attack that position.

Stalemate is a powerful technique for saving a lost or inferior endgame. Stalemates arise mainly due to a mistake. A player ignores a defensive action and leaves one or more sacrificial pieces on a silver plate to hit the desired location.

Conclusion

Knowing the most important chess terminology is vital for any beginner. Now that the mystery about chess stalemate has been cleared up, keep an eye out for ways to use and take advantage of these ideas! Stalemate is a valuable defensive resource, if you have a poor or even hopeless situation.

Chess endgame tips

Chess can be divided into three stages: beginning, middle game, and endgame. However, beginner chess players often devote much of their time to good opening play and tactics, avoiding the "boring" positional themes associated with long-term strategy and chess endgame motifs. The value of endgame comprehension and chess strategy should not be overlooked, as the vast majority of chess games do not end in opening or middle game.

It is all too normal that all-level chess players do not pay enough attention to the value of developing precise endgame strategy, resulting in missed opportunities and corresponding feelings of dissatisfaction and embarrassment.

The following 7 beginner chess endgame tips will get you the smallest endgame advantages in no time!

Lack of proper endgame technique allows many players to escape from lost positions, even without any spectacular play on their part" – Leonid Shamkovich

Chess endgame technique #1: piece activity

First of all the idea of piece operation is extremely important in any chess endgame.

Are your opponent's pieces tied to defending passively? Do you have open files or outposts for your pieces? Try to reach for an aggressive configuration of your pieces and avoid passive positions.

Piece operation also trumps material in the endgame: If you can, optimize the power of your pieces and make them as active as possible. Even at the expense of a little bit of material, this can significantly boost your place and allow you to win games that might not have seemed winnable at first.

The content is sometimes not as important as the initiative in endgames. Therefore, let all your pieces participate in the endgame and improve all your pieces to the squares where they have the most effect. Do not forget to play with all of your bits.

There is one more chess endgame secret about successful piece play. Do not only determine the position of your own pieces, but also your opponent's pieces.

Chess endgame technique #2: king activity

Endgames are radically different from middle games. King's changing position is one of the most significant characteristics distinguishing endgames from middle games and openings. The king must be well secured in opening and sharp middle game positions. However once you hit an endgame, the subject of king operation becomes paramount. An active king can protect vulnerabilities and control important squares so that more valuable pieces like rooks can be positioned more actively and need not perform defensive tasks. However, blindly upholding these chess endgame concepts is key. You can see the tips as guidelines to support you in most endgames, but they cannot apply to every scenario – remember to calculate. Centralizing the king does not make sense in any endgame: for example, if you have a queen endgame, you need to verify whose king is safer.

Chess endgame technique #3: pawn structure

Pawn structures play a key endgame role. Compare your pawn structure with your opponent's pawn structure. Is the pawn form symmetrical? Has your opponent poor pawns or squares? How many islands do you have? Are pawns moved or doubled? All these questions must be answered in the endgame. With reduced endgame content, pawn vulnerabilities like doubled pawns, isolated pawns, backward pawns, several pawn islands, etc. can turn out to be decisive factors. Therefore, avoiding reckless pawn moves in the endgame is key. Remember: pawns will move forward, but never backwards. If your pawn is bad try not to trade too many pieces. The more pieces coming off the board, the more pawn vulnerabilities start counting. Good endgame technique helps you to exploit the vulnerabilities in your opponent's position.

Chess endgame technique #4: realize critical changes in the position

Some decisions are irreversible in chess. For example, piece exchanges cannot be retrieved. Although this can be extended to all stages of the game, it is particularly important in the endgame because as less material remains, each exchange becomes more meaningful. Pay attention to all possible long-term position changes, particularly pawn structures and any minor piece exchanges. Of course, there are other essential factors to remember such as initiative, attack, heavy piece exchanges, etc. – But the key argument here is as more pieces become exchanged in a chess game, the value of the remaining pieces increases. That is why you have to think twice about which endgame pieces to swap. Because of the reduced endgame stuff, it is even more important than middle games. Make sure you share good bits.

Chess endgame technique #5: patience is a virtue – do not hurry

If you travel too quickly and make errors, it is not conducive to success. Time management is one thing, but impulse-taking bits is another. This idea applies even more in the endgame – because there are so many subtle tricks that can shift the result from win to draw, or from draw to lose.

Although you won't generally have a lot of time left in the endgame, you can still use a careful approach to ensure you won't let your opponent slip out of a bad place. Do not play too quickly on the clock or board, as steady improvement would certainly be better than loose tactical holes movements.

"Patience is the most valuable trait of the endgame player" – Pal Benko

Here are the 3 key chess endgame rules of patient play:

- Slow, consistent endgame play is important. Do not rush in quiet positions: if the enemy is deprived of aggressive counter play, aim to strengthen your position before any concrete action begins. Do not bother winning as fast as possible. Look for the game's best qualitatively.
- Make no promises for good cause. Play patiently and slowly change.
- Grouping the pieces to useful squares is the best realistic endgames technique. Sometimes, your opponents won't be able to manage your sluggish, careful play and weaken their position even more quickly.

Chess endgame technique #6: schematic thinking – form a plan

Technique becomes foundamental in endgames. Most realistic endgames involve thought in terms of schedules. Pure variance estimation does not help handle most endgames.

You must also strive to grasp the position's basics thoroughly. Only this helps you to prepare the next 5-10 moves or more.

Schematic thought is important. Thinking in schemes means thinking in small plan elements. Therefore you must first identify your overall strategy.

An overall strategic plan can for example, encourage an extra pawn on one side of the board or gain a weak pawn. However this target normally involves a lot of preparatory work. You need to come up with some small plans including improving the pieces' position, centralizing the king, establishing a kingside vulnerability, advancing pawns, suppressing counter play, etc. If you are not sure how exactly you can improve your endgame position, it is good to start by improving your worst-placed piece.

Chess endgame technique #7: tactics in the endgame

Apparently easy endgames can be shockingly tactical. For example, there are occasions to checkmate. If your opponent's king looks weak, see if you can take away squares and trap them. In addition, chess endgame strategies are paramount when transforming the accumulated advantages. Most of the time, finishing the game needs a tactical blow to make the advantage more concrete. Effective endgame technique and chess tactics also go hand-in-hand.

Conclusion

Many of the realistic endgame tactics discussed in this article appear to replicate. These tactics can be seen as guides that you can use to maneuvers more confidently through every endgame in your games. For this reason, you should consider these endgame tactics as a mental toolbox that lets you play good moves whenever endgames occur.

HOW TO DECIDE YOUR NEXT CHESS MOVE

Chess is a decision game. On the chessboard, we do not only see what we play. Imagine playing an important game in a chess tournament, and you have reached a victory, but a difficult situation with a little time left on the clock. Let's say you have at your disposal four promising chess movements that seem good at first sight. However on closer analysis, it turns out that only one move wins. In such a scenario, you must decide quickly and play the right move to win the game.

If you play another move that seems to be similarly solid, but actually loses the game due to some shift order nuances, it won't help you say after the end of the game that you considered playing the correct shift. You cannot change your game decision afterwards.

Step 1: Figure out the key elements of the position and define your plan.

Step 2: Consider your opponent's plans, threats, and his last move.

Step 3: Come up with candidate moves for your next chess move.

Step 4: Calculate your next chess move (calculate forcing moves first, check the move order, blunder-checking).

Step 5: Execute your next chess move.

To explain this main feature, we will dive into an example and discuss the aspects involved

To learn the most from this example, we suggest you stop reading and try to solve this puzzle first. Moving is white. Can you spot white's winning combination?

White's place at hand looks promising as black's king is stuck in the corner and has no escape squares. White's most rational move here would be 1Qh1+ (always try to calculate forcing chess moves like checks and captures first). However the problem with this move is black's resource 1...d5+. Not only does black block the diagonal, he gives himself a check with his queen.

Black will take the pawn on a7 with 2...Kxa7 after a chess move like 2.Ka5, and no more mating risks. Another suggestion for white is playing 1.Nd5, blocking d-pawn and threatening b6 and c7 mate. But once white's knight moves, black will check d3 (1...Qd3) and white loses his knight.

Moreover, there are also more chess movements for white to consider as 1.Qh8 (pinning the knight on f8), 1.Nc6 (blocking the 6th rank) or 1.Qc2 (threatening to swap queens and mate black's king with the knight).

The only winning move is 1.Qh6!! White threatens to take black's queen on g6 and take black's knight on f8. White's queen, however, is not secured on h6 – black can take it with 1...Qxh6. Yet white's heavy movement – 2Nd5 (see the diagram on the left). The knight blocks d6's pawn. Black has no check with his queen and cannot defend the next move against the mate.

Notice that after a chess move like 1...Qf5, eliminating the queen and defending the knight on f8, white has 2.Qh1+! Since black's queen left 6th, the move...d5 no longer comes with a review.

After 2...d5, white wins after 3.Qxd5+ Qxd5 4.Nxd5 and black gets matched, as his king cannot escape from the a8-square. In a realistic game, the decision that chess moves to play next (1.Qh1+, 1.Nd5, 1.Qc2, 1.Qh8 or 1.Qh6) determines on the game outcome – in the last case white wins; in the other cases, white just draws or even loses.

Deciding your next chess move

As we have seen, determining your next chess move in a game is not always easy. Chess players sometimes blunder, making the wrong decision. The key distinction between grandmasters and ordinary club players is that they are qualified to make decisions and have far more practical skills. Many club players spend much energy measuring chess movements that grandmasters simply overlook because they know these movements are evil. As a result, many players waste precious time on poor chess moves and strategies, later in the game losing time for important decisions.

Candidate chess moves:

"It is seeing before you thought. In the first three seconds, we all find two or three ideas in every place. However, we are not guaranteed they are the best. If we train to look for additional ideas, we will end up with a list of interesting moves that make sense to quantify."

Finding the correct candidate chess move is one of the toughest aspects of being a better chess player. Naturally, choosing the right candidate move depends on the position's existence. You may develop candidate movements based on intuition, pattern recognition, estimation, guessing, strategic and positional concepts and several more approaches.

The most successful way to find the right candidate moves is to include the following factors of your reasoning process when determining your next move:

What is the important elements of the position: Material, pawn structures, upper and lower minor pieces, space, initiative, king protection, control of important files or squares, vulnerabilities may be key factors.

What is your plan: Do you want to launch an assault on the opponent's king? Do you want to target many vulnerabilities in your opponent's camp? Do you want to swap queens, as this would be nice for you? It is always important to know what to do. If this question is not answered, you should take your time and describe your job strategy.

What does your opponent last move imply? Chess is a game involving opposition. Since you are not the only one who plans to win the game, your opponent might try to trick you or set traps for you. To get better at chess, it is important not only to concentrate on your own plans, but also to look out for the plans and threats of your opponent.

What is the drawback of my opponent's last chess move? It is important to understand that as long as they are on the square, both chess pieces and pawns control those squares. Once they move, they control new squares, but still give up some other squares. This definition is particularly useful for pawn moves. As we all know, pawns cannot go backwards. If you start your game with 1.f4, you will get control over the important central square e5, but you will also weaken your king's position, which now has less of a defending pawn.

Calculate forcing moves first: Forcing chess moves, as the name implies, is easier to quantify because they compel the opponent to play those moves. If you search, your opponent has to do something instantly about it – he cannot avoid it for one or two moves and play an intermediate chess game. If you catch the queen of your enemy, he typically has to recover, as otherwise he would be significantly down on material. Instead if you calculate a quiet chess move, your opponent has different moves to play.

Check your move: Often you see an interesting tactical prospect, but the combination does not seem to work. In these situations, changing the movement order is a highly successful process. If you start the move you wanted to play second or third, you can try if your combination works. Quite often, shifting order makes a difference.

"Some people keep wondering after choosing what they want to do. The less evident downside is that at times they just change their minds to pick moves below their first decision! Even if they stop this, they later end in time trouble. .''

Since you do not have infinite time to perform your chess movements in a realistic game, you have to stop thinking at some stage and just pass. If you think 30 minutes on which of your two rooks to place on an open file in moving 10, you will lose this time in a complicated situation that can arise after moving 20.

PART TWO

THE GAME OF CHESS.

Today, the game of chess is played by two people and is known for difficult maneuvering and strategic planning all over the world. You can learn and have a good time playing the basics of chess, or you can learn chess notation and learn how the world's great players think. Chess's goal is to maneuver your pieces in an effort to remove the pieces of your opponent and eventually capture his or her king. That might sound easy enough, but do not forget that your opponent has the same goal in mind, so you also have to strategize your defense while strategizing for your win. In chess, there are some difficult and fast rules, but there is also an art of achieving the ultimate goal of "checkmate" (winning the game). In the motion of your pieces, the art is in the way you strategize the win.

No secret knowledge is involved in the play. It starts with 16 pieces for each player: one king, one queen, two rooks, two knights, two bishops, and eight pawns. Each type of piece moves differently, with the queen being the most powerful and the pawn the least powerful. The goal is to checkmate the king of the opponent by putting it under an inescapable capture threat. To this end, the pieces of a player are used to strike and catch the pieces of the enemy, thus supporting each other. Play usually includes trading pieces for the comparable pieces of the opponent during the game, and seeking and engineering opportunities to exchange beneficially or to get a better position. In addition to checkmate, if the opponent resigns, a player wins the game or runs out of time in a timed game. There are many ways a game can end in a draw, as well.

Chess strategy consists of creating and gaining long-term positioning advantages throughout the game, such as where various pieces are positioned, whereas strategies focus on immediate maneuvering. It is not possible to distinguish these two aspects of the gameplay entirely, since strategic objectives are often accomplished by tactics, whereas tactical opportunities are based on the previous strategy of play. A chess game is generally divided into three phases: the beginning, normally the first 10 moves, when players shift their pieces to useful positions for the battle to come; the middle game; and the final game, when most of the pieces are gone, kings usually take a more active part in the combat, and the promotion of the pawn is always decisive.

Chess is fun, and you can have fun with chess! However, many people do not have particularly fond memories of their first chess moves. You probably have a lot of misconceptions about the game, unless you are a professional chess player.

You may think that chess players are smart people, or that intelligence is associated with learning to play chess well. You may think that chess is hard, or that you are hopelessly not good, and it is an impossible task to defeat that friend or relative who is the reigning champion consistently. Maybe you think that chess is dull, that it is an activity for which you are not well equipped. The truth is that chess, from the beginning, can and should be stimulating and enjoyable and inspiring. It is inherently interactive, and while it is a zero-sum competition over the board, a set of tractable tasks that include a means of self-improvement and social interaction are more relevant.

The history of the chess game.

The history of chess among historians is a much-debated topic, but the consensus is that it has its roots in Persia or India. A 4,000-year-old game called Chaturanga, a game played with dice and pieces consisting of elephants, horses, chariots, and foot soldiers, is the oldest ancestor of chess. The most recent ancestor of chess, as we know it today, is a 2,000-year-old game played by Persians and Arabs called "Shatranj." A champion player of his day (1840's) named Howard Staunton designed the modern game of Chess.

In ancient Afrasiab, today's Samarkand, in Uzbekistan, Central Asia, the oldest prehistoric chess objects, ivory pieces, have been excavated and date to around 760, with some of them probably older. The oldest known chess manual was written in Arabic and dates from 840-850, by al-Adli ar-Rumi (800-870), a renowned Arab chess player, named The Chess Book. This is a missing manuscript, but cited in subsequent works. There is also less data on the eastern migration of chess to China and Southeast Asia than on its migration to west. In a book entitled "Record of the Mysterious and Strange" dated to around 800, the first reference to Chinese chess appears. Alternatively, some argue that, although this has been disputed, chess originated from Chinese chess or one of its predecessors.

In southern Europe, the rules of shatranj began to be changed around 1200, and around 1475, several significant changes rendered the game basically as it is today known. In Italy and Spain, these modern laws were introduced for simple gestures. Pawns gained the opportunity on their first move to advance two squares, while bishops and queens learned their modern skills.

By the end of the 10th century, the queen replaced the earlier vizier chess piece, and by the 15th century it had become the most powerful piece; modern chess was therefore referred to as "Queen's Chess" or "Mad Queen Chess" Castling, originating from the kings' leap, was usually implemented in conjunction with a pawn or rook move to bring the king to safety. These new laws have spread rapidly all over Western Europe.

Chess first appeared around the 6th century AD in India and had spread from Asia to the Middle East and Europe by the 10th century. Chess has been regarded as the "royal game" since at least the 15th century due to its prominence among the aristocracy. Slowly, rules and set design progressed until each achieved the standard of today in the early 19th century. Formerly an intellectual diversion preferred by the upper classes, as elite and state-sponsored players played for an officially recognized world championship title and increasingly lucrative tournament prizes, chess went through an exponential rise in interest throughout the 20th century. Men, women, and children all over the world are now fascinated by organized chess competitions, postal correspondence games, and internet chess.

There are several claims going around today that chess did not originate in Persia or India, but rather in China, with some very solid evidence to support them. Other scholars also contend that chess was invented by ancient women and that the game is simply one of fertility and procreation rather than war and combat.

Ancient precursors and related games

A matter of debate remains as to the roots of chess. There is no reliable evidence that prior to the 6th century CE, chess existed in a form resembling the modern game. Game pieces found in Russia, China, India, Central Asia, Pakistan, and elsewhere that have been determined to be older than that are now known to come from previous board games that are distantly related, sometimes involving dice and often using 100 or more square boards.

A war game called chaturanga, a Sanskrit name for a battle formation mentioned in the Indian epic Mahabharata, was one of those earlier games. By the 7th century, Chaturanga flourished in northwestern India and is considered the earliest ancestor of modern chess since it had two main characteristics found in all later chess variants. Different pieces had different forces (unlike checkers and go and victory was based on one piece, the modern chess king. It is unknown how chaturanga evolved. Some historians claim that chaturanga, probably played on a 64-square board with dice, gradually turned into shatranj (or chatrang), a two-player game common after 600 CE in northern India, Pakistan, Afghanistan, and southern Central Asia. Shatranj was similar to chaturanga, but he added a new piece, a firzān (counsellor), which had little to do with the formation of any troops. A shatranj game could be won either by eliminating all of the pieces of an opponent (baring the king) or by ensuring the king's capture. The initial positions of the pawns and knights did not change, but the other pieces had major regional and temporal variations.

The game spread to the east, north and west, assuming sharply different features. It was transformed into a game with inscribed discs in the East, carried by Buddhist pilgrims, Silk Road traders, and others who were often positioned at the intersection of the board lines rather than inside the squares. Chess reached China about 750 CE, and by the 11th century it had reached Japan and Korea. The most popular variant of the Eastern game, Chinese chess, has 9 files and 10 ranks as well as a river border between the 5th and 6th ranks, which restricts access to the enemy camp and makes the game slower than its Western cousin.

Introduction to Europe

By the 10th century, Muslims had taken chess to North Africa, Sicily, and Spain. It was distributed by the Eastern Slavs to Kievan Rus at the same time. The Vikings took the game as far as Iceland and England and are believed to be responsible for the most popular array of chessmen, 78 pieces of walrus-ivory from different sets found in the Outer Hebrides in 1831 on the Isle of Lewis and dated from the 11th or 12th century. Kings and religious figures occasionally banned chess and dice games. For instance, in 1254, King Louis IX prohibited the game in France. The popularity of the game however was supported by its social cachet: a chess set was often connected with money, experience, and influence. It was a favorite of England's Kings Henry I, Henry II, John, and Richard I, of Spain's Philip II and Alfonso X (the Wise), and of Russia's Ivan IV (The Terrible). As early as the 15th century, it was known as the royal game.

Standardization of chess rules

Slowly, with widespread regional variation, the current rules and appearance of chess pieces evolved. By 1300, for instance, on its first turn, the pawn had gained the ability to move two squares, rather than just one at a time as it did in shatranj. However, for more than 300 years, this law has not earned general acceptance in Europe. After two important rule changes that became common after 1475, chess made its greatest progress. Until then the advisor was limited to diagonally changing one square at a time. In addition, since only a counsellor could become a pawn who achieved eighth rank, pawn promotion was a relatively minor factor in the course of a game. However, the counsellor underwent a sex shift under the new rules and acquired vastly improved mobility to become the modern monarch, the most influential piece on the board. A complex new feature was introduced to chess through this and the increased value of pawn promotion. In addition, the bishop became the chaturanga piece formerly called the elephant, which was limited to a two-square diagonal jump in shatranj, more than doubling its length. Checkmate was relatively uncommon before these changes happened, and more frequently a game was determined by barring the king. The trench warfare of medieval chess was replaced by a game in which a checkmate could be delivered in as few as two moves with the modern queen and bishop forces. It took longer to gain approval for the last two big changes in the rules, castling and en passant capture. In the 15th century, both laws were known but had limited use until the 18th century. Minor differences in other rules persisted until the late 19th century; for example, if a player still had the original queen, it was not permissible in certain parts of Europe as late as the mid-19th century to promote a pawn to a queen.

Set design

Since the days of chaturanga, the appearance of chess pieces has alternated between plain and ornate. Before 600 CE, the simplistic design of pieces gradually led to figurative sets that portrayed animals, warriors, and noblemen. However, after the Islamic prohibition of depictions of living beings, Muslim sets of the 9th-12th centuries were mostly non-representative and made of plain clay or carved stone. It is believed that the return to simpler, symbolic shatranj pieces spurred the popularity of the game by making sets easier to make and by redirecting the attention of the players from the complex pieces to the game itself. As the game spread to Europe and Russia, stylized collections, mostly decorated with precious and semi-precious stones, returned to fashion. Playing boards, which in the Muslim world had monochromatic squares, started to have alternating squares of black and white, or red and white, by 1000 CE and were mostly made of fine wood or marble. Russia's Peter I (the Great) had unique campaign boards that he carried during military activities made of soft leather.

The king acquires a crown and often an intricate throne and mace, being the largest item. The close identification of the knight with the horse dates back to Chaturanga. The pawn has historically been the smallest and least representational of the pieces, as the lowest in power and social status. After 1475, as its forces increased, the queen grew in size and shifted from a male advisor to the female consort of the king. The bishop was addressed by various names, such as "fool" in French and "elephant" in Russian, and a distinctive miter was not widely recognised until the 19th century.

The depiction of the tower also differed greatly. Up until the 20th century, it was commonly portrayed in Russia as a sailing ship. Elsewhere in a chariot or castle turret, there was a knight. Around 1835, with a simple design by an Englishman, Nathaniel Cook, the standard for modern sets was developed. The design was endorsed by Howard Staunton, then the world's best player, after it was patented in 1849; it eventually became known as the Staunton pattern due to Staunton's widespread promotion. In global competition today, only sets based on the Staunton design are permitted.

Past world championship

Over the past two centuries, chess' popularity has been strongly tied to rivalry, typically in the form of two-player matches, for World Champion title. Until 1886, the title was unofficial, but widespread spectator interest in the game started over 50 years earlier. The first major international event was a series of six matches between Paris' leading French and British clubs, Louis-Charles de la Bourdonnais, and London's Alexander McDonnell, which ended with Bourdonnais' victory. A major chess event was first widely published in newspapers and studied in books. After Bourdonnais' death in 1840, Staunton succeeded him after another match attracting international attention, Staunton's 1843 defeat of France's Pierre-Charles Fournier de Saint-Amant. This match also helped introduce the concept of stakes rivalry, as Staunton received 100 from both players' backers.

Staunton used his role as an unofficial world champion in popularizing the Staunton-pattern set, advocating a standardized set of rules, and organizing the first international tournament in London in 1851. Karl Ernst Adolf Anderssen, a German schoolteacher, was motivated by the Bourdonnais-McDonnell match to switch from problem-setting to tournament rivalry, winning the London tournament and acknowledging it as unofficial champion. The London tournament, in turn encouraged American players to organize the First American Chess Congress in New York City in 1857, which set off the Western Hemisphere's first chess craze. New Orleans' winner Paul Morphy was known as unofficial world champion after beating Anderssen in 1858.

The world championship became more formalised after Morphy retired and in 1866, Wilhelm Steinitz of Prague beat Anderssen. Steinitz was the first to assert authority to decide how to hold a title match. He set a series of rules and financial conditions under which he would defend his position as the world's leading player, and in 1886 he agreed to play versus Austria's Johann Zukertort in the first game specifically designated as World Championship. Steinitz reserved the right to decide his challenge and when and how frequently he would defend his title. Steinitz's successor, Germany's Emanuel Lasker, proved more demanding than Steinitz in organizing matches did. From 1897 to 1907 and later from 1910 to 1921, he took long stretches without defending his title. After the leading national chess federations, British and German, failed to organize a match on the eve of World War I between Lasker and some of his leading challengers, the moment for independent international authority began to rise.

The championship controversy was eased when Cuba's José Raúl Capablanca beat Lasker in 1921 and won a written set of rules for championship challenges at a London tournament in 1922 from the world's other leading players. Under those rules, any player meeting certain financial conditions (especially guaranteeing a $10,000 stake) may challenge the World Champion. Although the top players tried to stick to the London Rules, members of fifteen countries met in 1924 in Paris to organise the first permanent international chess federation, known as FIDE, its French acronym for Fédération Internationale des Échecs.

The London Rules worked smoothly in 1927 when Alexander Alekhine, the first Russian-born champion, dethroned Capablanca, but then proved a financial barrier in Capablanca's bid for a rematch. FIDE's attempted interference failed. Alekhine was widely blamed for manipulating the rules and FIDE claimed power to arrange world championship matches when he died in 1946.

The FIDE format worked without major problems from 1948, when FIDE organized a match tournament to fill the vacancy created by Alekhine's death. The international federation arranged three-year cycles of regional and international competitions to decide World Champion challengers and requested match site bids. The champion was no longer vetoing rivals and had to defend the title every three years.

Development of theory

There are three known phases in a chess game: opening, where piece production and center control predominate; middle game, where defense maneuvering and attacking the opponent's king or vulnerabilities occurs; and endgame, where pawn promotion becomes the dominant theme usually after many piece exchanges. Chess theory involves knowledge opening, tactics (or combinations), positional analysis (particularly pawn structures), strategy (making long-range plans and goals), and endgame technique (including basic mates against the lone king).

The birth of chess theory

Early chess players realized that a standard game could be divided into three stages, each with its own character and priorities: the opening stage, where a player creates the pieces from their starting squares; a middle game stage, where strategies are formulated and executed; and an endgame stage, after many trades and catches, in which the superior chances player attempts to devise.

Analyzing some basic opening movements, elementary middle game variations, and simple endgame technique elements appeared as early as the 15th century. Around 1620 an Italian master, Gioacchino Greco, wrote an overview of a sequence of composed games highlighting two opposing chess approaches. Those games pit a player who tries to win as many of the opponent's pieces as possible against an opponent who loses material in search of checkmate—and typically wins. Greco, the first chess professional, stressed tactics. His games were packed with pretty variations of bad defensive play. They had great impact in popularizing chess and showing various ideas on how to play it.

François-André Philidor of France arrived in the 18th century to describe how chess games are won. Philidor, a music composer, has been the world's greatest chess player for almost 50 years. In 1749, Philidor wrote and published L'Analyze des échecs (Chess Analyzed), an influential book that appeared in over 100 editions.

Philidor used seemingly fictional games in examine to demonstrate his principles for fighting a political, not military war. Other masters copied his remarks on some 1e4 e5 openings for decades, and his study of king, queen, and bishop against king and rook was the first thorough review of a single endgame. Yet

Philidor's middlegame guidance was his biggest legacy. He emphasised the planning role: once all pieces of a player are created, that player should try to shape an overall target, such as kingside attack, that coordinates forces. Philidor also put an emphasis on predicting enemy attacks, rather than only relying on one's own attack.

Greco and previous authors discussed two or three pieces' tactical interplay. Yet Philidor assumed that pawns' meaning had been ignored, calling special attention to their vulnerabilities and strengths. His most popular comment—that "peonies are the very life of the game"—is frequently quoted without specifying why they are important: because, he said, pawns alone form the base for the attack.

Philidor assumed that the middle game's most significant positional element is a mobile mass of pawns and that an attack would fail unless adequately supported by the pawns. He cautioned against allowing pawns to be separated, doubled on the same file, or rendered backward—that is, unguarded by another pawn and unable to safely advance. He related the characteristics of pawns to other pieces and was the first to highlight how a bishop could be bad or good, based on how small a set pawn structure was. He also proposed an f-pawn swap with an enemy e-pawn as it would partly open the register for a castled f1 rook. While previous scholars had shown how to temporarily sacrifice pawns or other pieces in checkmating or material-gaining configurations, Philidor explained the purely positional sacrifice under which a player obtains compensation, such as superior piece stability or pawn structure.

Morphy and the theory of attack

By studying the play of 16th-century Italian masters, the Modena school proved that games could be won in less than 20 moves by swift piece mobilization, contrasted with Philidor's slow-developing pawn marches.

There followed a plethora of speculative pawn sacrifices in the opening called gambits, in order to gain rapid mobilization and open lines for an attack. Checkmating attacks, often with surprising compromises in concluding combos, were the trademark of many players in the 19th century. These leading masters were described as part of the Romantic school of chess. The theories of the Modena school were not completely understood until they appeared, in slightly different form, in the games of Paul Morphy, the first American acknowledged as the world's best athlete. Morphy's chess career lasted less than three years and consisted of less than 75 serious games. In 1858–59 he beat all the leading European teams, with the disappointing exception of Howard Staunton, who evaded all attempts to arrange a match. At the age of 22 Morphy retired from serious chess. Morphy is the only great chess theorist who leaves no written legacy. Morphy's contemporaries learned as much about the openings as he did, and some of them could measure combinations as well as he. Yet Morphy knew how and when to attack better than anyone else. This allowed him not only to win favorable positions but also to prevent defeat in inferior positions. After he beat Adolf Anderssen, the greatest of the Romantics, by a lopsided score of 7–2, a supporter asked Anderssen why he had not lost his pieces beautifully against the American, as he had against other masters. "Morphy won't let me," Anderssen is reputed to have replied.

Morphy appreciated that superior development—getting pieces into good squares in the first 10 to 15 moves—was comparatively unimportant in the semi closed, blocked pawn systems that Philidor had adopted. However, as the center or kingside becomes more accessible, a benefit in growth grew in importance. In Morphy's best-known games, pawns and knights played small positions. Pawns were also sacrificed so that the queen, rooks, and bishops could join the attack as quickly as possible. The first goal for Morphy was the initiative, the desire to force mattered. Superior construction in a position with few center pawns bestowed the initiative on one player. In the games of lesser players the initiative could pass back and forth as players err. Yet Morphy rarely failed to put an idea to fruition.

Steinitz and the theory of equilibrium

Morphy's subsequent heir, Wilhelm Steinitz, reigned as world champion until 1894, when he was 58. The Prague-born Steinitz managed to maintain his dominance for so long because he established new concepts of the middle game, especially in closed or semi closed positions that only his successor, Emanuel Lasker, and Lasker's contemporaries truly understood. Steinitz said his "modern school" was motivated by two premises: first that the inevitable result of a game is a tie because of the intrinsic equilibrium between the powers of white and black and, second, that checkmate is the final but not the first goal of the game. Steinitz started his career as a pragmatic, combinational player in the Morphy style. However, in his late thirties he gained insight into subtle spatial characteristics that take precedence in positions in which the center is entirely or partly obscured by immobile pawns. Steinitz sought to resolve the question of why some attacks succeed, regardless of how skillful was the defender, and others fail, regardless of how brilliant the attacker was. A failed assault, he said, frequently results in failure for the attacker, whose forces unexpectedly become poorly organized in the face of a counterattack. Steinitz concluded that in a traditional situation each side has some minor advantages which help to balance one another. For example, a player could have weakened the opponent's pawns but at the cost of exchanging a bishop for a marginally less-valuable knight. An attack is acceptable only after the equilibrium has been upset, by either the player's faults or the opponent's successful moves. Morphy's advantage in growth was one way of disrupting the equilibrium. However, by the 1870s, after Morphy's games became common to all masters, it became harder and harder to achieve a lead in progress against a reluctant rival.

Steinitz found that the way to justify a decisive assault in the post-Morphy period was to accumulate slight, sometimes subtle, advantages—for example, having two bishops while one's opponent has two knights, having an entrenched knight at a fortified outpost, or having greater maneuvering space. In his games Steinitz demonstrated how slow-evolving maneuvers in the opening, especially with knights, paid dividends in the middle game if the center was closed. He originated the word "hole" to denote a weak square that has lost its pawn defense and can be filled favorably by an enemy piece.

Although a lead in development could be temporary, other benefits, such as a superior pawn structure, may be nurtured into the endgame, Steinitz said. Structural vulnerabilities usually include pawns that are difficult to defend or squares (especially in the center or around the king) that enemy pieces can occupy without being dislodged by pawn attacks. The following typical pawn vulnerabilities are disadvantageous in direct proportion to their exploitability, which continues to increase as pieces are traded. A pawn with no friendly pawns on adjoining files is called an isolated pawn; isolated pawns can confer middle game compensation by control of important squares (if placed in the center) or by giving rooks adjoining open files along which to strike. A pawn on an open file whose progress is restrained by an enemy pawn on an adjoining file and who is unguidable by any other pawn is called a backward pawn. Two pawns that share the same file (through captures) are called doubled pawns. The minor advantages could be translated at a suitable moment to material by means of attack. He added that a player who does not attack while in a spot favorable enough to warrant it would risk the advantage.

Unlike the Romantics, who aggressively shot for the enemy king, Steinitz concluded that the essence of the situation determined whether to attack the kingside or queenside. The victory of a single pawn was in the vast majority of cases fatal among first-class masters.

Any subtle advantages do not become important until the endgame, Steinitz found. For example, after regular pawn captures and recaptures, a player is always left with three pawns each on the kingside and queenside, while the opponent has four on the kingside and two on the queenside. The kingside pawns are sometimes kept back near or on their original squares for king defense. However, advancing on the queenside where the player has a majority of the pawns, referred to as a queenside majority, will produce a strong passing pawn that may prove decisive in the late middle game or endgame. In the other hand, one of Steinitz's students, Harry Nelson Pillsbury, popularized the "minority attack," in which the player with less queenside pawns advances them in some positions in order to weaken his opponent's pawns.

Steinitz was also the first master of defensive play. In addition, when playing the white pieces, he always invited his opponent to open the center by exchanging pawns or to be the first to cross the fourth rank. He reasoned that such attacks would be premature if the equilibrium was in balance and so should be punished after careful defensive play. Although Philidor was known for his writings and Morphy for his games, Steinitz left a legacy to both. In match play he regularly beat the leading Romantics—Adolf Anderssen, Joseph Blackburne, Johann Zukertort, and Mikhail Chigorin. He is regarded as the first player to pursue a theoretical approach to chess.

The classical era

Among Steinitz's biggest supporters were two Germans, Emanuel Lasker and Siegbert Tarrasch. Lasker dethroned Steinitz as world champion in 1894 and improved his philosophy of defensive play. He demonstrated that even crowded positions yielded good counterattacking opportunities. Often, he was the first player to understand the psychological essence of chess and found that by taking supposedly poor positions or those with merely weaker pawn systems, he put a psychological pressure on many of his opponents by promoting their confidence. His realistic approach to the game helped Lasker to retain the world championship title until 1921. Still as a later world champion, Max Euwe, said of him, "It is not possible to learn much from him; one can only stand and wonder."

Tarrasch put Steinitz's principles in a different way. He viewed the control of space and versatility of pieces as much more important than Steinitz claimed and thought that these qualities would compensate for structural pawn vulnerabilities. He was the champion of a specific pawn structure containing an independent d-pawn. Steinitz saw such a pawn as a liability that could be advantageously blockaded by an enemy knight and ultimately caught. But Tarrasch observed that the same pawn could support one or two of his own knights on more advanced squares, and this always outweighed the obvious vulnerability. His games display a constant attempt to get all his pieces on their best squares and to take possession of more space. This led Tarrasch to original attitudes toward stuff, such as claiming that two bishops and a rook were approximately equal to two rooks and a knight. He disliked the cramped positions that Lasker perfected and relished.

Tarrasch chose to use a superior centre to strike on both wings of the board at the same time. As the world's leading chess author for over three decades, Tarrasch popularised Steinitz's results, mostly by restricting them to simplistic rules like "develop knights before bishops" or do not move your queen early in the game."

Capablanca finally dethroned Lasker, who added little to the game theory, but showed how Steinitz and Tarrasch's teachings could be molded into an almost unbeatable formula. Capablanca perfected the skill players call technique, fostering tiny advantages until they become decisive. Capablanca paid little attention to the opening and played both 1 e4, master's favourite until about 1910, and 1 d4, a move likely to keep the center closed. He preferred clear-cut middle games. But he argued that each move, even in the opening, should go beyond that goal—a contrast with Morphy, who appeared to develop pieces for development.

Capablanca created a play style that allowed him to minimise risk; he went eight years, from 1916 to 1924, without losing a tournament or match game. Other leading players, including Akiba Rubinstein and Carl Schlechter, developed their own minimal-risk strategies when attempting to perfect Steinitz's theories. Material advantage became a priority. Frequency sacrifices declined, and gambits nearly disappeared at master level. The absence of new ideas in chess was reflected in the appearance of agreed draws in less than 20 moves—ironically called "grandmaster draws"—in the 20th century's first two decades.

Hyper modernism

After World War I, a major chess school emerged with an assault by Central European masters on Steinitz's approach to the center and Tarrasch's dogmatic rules. The Hypermodernists, as they were known, were delighted to show how to profitably violate previous generation guidelines. In one of his favorite openings, Aron Nimzowitsch began three pawn advances, followed by his queen's move. His colleague Richard Réti wrote that the younger generation was interested in exceptions, not laws. The main exceptions were center squares, mainly e4, e5, d4, and d5. The Hypermodernists believed the central pawn structure was a goal since Philidor could be a liability because it provides a target to the opponent. The center's occupation was not desirable, but its control, they argued. Gyula Breyer, one of the Hypermodernists, summed up their approach by joking, "white's game is in the last throes after the first move."

The opening was at the heart of hyper modernism. The two new school leaders, Réti and Nimzowitsch, attacked Tarrasch's emphasis on building a solid centre in the first dozen moves, starting with 1 e4 or 1 d4. Réti often started a game with 1 Nf3 and did not advance more than one pawn before the middle game started. Instead, he and the other Hypermodernists rediscovered fianchetto, or bishop development on its longest diagonal—i.e., b2 and g2 for white, b7 and g7 for black. Fianchettoed bishops were Howard Staunton's favorite in the 1830s, but fell out of favor after Morphy popularized open centers. Réti's plan was to strike the middle with bits on wings. In one of his most divisive maneuvers, he moved his queen to a1 to highlight b2's bishop's control.

The Hypermodern invited their rivals to advance the middle pawns and often sought to taunt them. For example, Alexander Alekhine, a future world champion who pursued hypermodern concepts in the 1920s, created an opening that consisted of meeting 1 e4 with 1...Nf6 to tempt white to move to e5, where the pawn could later be shot. Nimzowitsch also played in the opening. Previously, masters replied 1 d4 almost immediately with 1...d5 to keep white from dominating the 2 e4 center. However, Nimzowitsch played 1...Nf6 with the intention of controlling the critical e4 square with small pieces, a white knight bishop pin at c3 and/or a fianchettoed bishop at b7. His schemes, known as the Queen's Indian Defense, remain among the most common in competitive play.

Nimzowitsch's discovery of opportunities previously exploited and found wanting led to another hypermodern tenet: the center's voluntary surrender. Steinitz believed this concept emerged, but Nimzowitsch expanded on it in many games and writings. A typical pawn chain, for example, occurs in the middle when white pawns occupy d4 and e5 and black pawns occupy d5 and e6. Tarrasch demonstrated how black gets counter chances by hitting the enemy center by advancing c-pawn to c5 and f-pawn to f6. Tarrasch's opponents managed to hold white pawns on their squares. However, Nimzowitsch sought the right time to swap white pawns (dxc5 and after...f6, then exf6). His goal was to fill deserted squares with his minor pieces at d4 and e5—i.e., bishops and knights.

Nimzowitsch also inspired the development of defensive prophylaxis ideas—anticipation, avoidance, and inhibition of the opponent's play.

The time element and competition

Origin of time controls

The advent of competitive chess with the 1834 Bourdonnais-McDonnell match and the 1851 London tournament raised a question of fairness: could a player take large quantities of time? Previously, chess had an unwritten amateur right that gave players unlimited time for each move. When the tradition of tracking the amount of time taken for each move in major events started, it was discovered that the 1843 Staunton–Saint-Amant match games averaged nine hours, and one player spent as much as two hours and 20 minutes on one move at the London tournament.

Staunton, the most successful player of the first half of the 19th century, was heavily critical of players who took "hours over moves where minutes might be enough." He proposed restricting the time available for each move to a given amount of minutes. But most officials accepted that some moves deserve lengthy attention, others very few. Since a player could not hold wasted time, he would be advised to take as many as possible. But encouraging a player to spend as much as 10 minutes per move would mean it will take two hours to play only six moves. The idea of one-step time limits was abolished in all but postal games (where players have a predetermined number of days to react to a move) and certain types of fast or speed chess—for example, games where players have to move every 5 or 10 seconds.

A second principle, also called sudden death, was also considered—and abandoned—in competitive chess early days. In a sudden-death format, a fixed period of time is required in a game for all a player's moves. Sudden-death time limits were deemed overly limiting in the 19th century and much of the 20th because they could leave a player with a massive edge, but so little time left that defeat was imminent. Sudden death survived only in such pace chess forms, such as five-minute chess, where each player has five minutes for all moves.

Tassilo von Heydebrand und der Lasa, a German player and author from the 19th century, suggested the third and most common theory for time controls. Lasa recommended allowing each player to play a predetermined number of moves, such as two hours for 30 moves. This theory, implemented from 1861 on by the vast majority of tournaments, encourages each player to budget time, play certain moves quickly and take as many as an hour or more on others. Additionally, a player who made the prescribed number of moves, like 30 in the above case, will get an extra time budget, such as one hour for the next 15 moves. Staunton had recommended that the punishment for exceeding a timeline be a fine, and this was attempted in some international competitions as late as Nürnberg 1906. However, as deterrent, this proved ineffective, and dismissal ultimately became the only punishment. After Vienna 1882, where a first-prize contender, James Mason, missed the time limit in one game but ultimately won the game after his rival failed to demand the forfeit. Another first-prize candidate, Wilhelm Steinitz, appealed Mason's victory and instead levied a forfeiture.

Technology improvement

In 1861 the first time limits, using hourglasses, were employed in a contest, Anderssen versus Ignác Kolisch, and in a tournament, at Bristol, England. Each player had a timer to put in motion before considering a move and to stop after the move. However, hourglasses proved clumsy and inexact and were replaced by a pair of mechanical clocks after a simple pendulum mechanism was introduced at London 1883. The pendulum operated as a seesaw so that when a player depressed his clock, it stopped and the opponent's clock started ticking.

Modern clocks consist of two parallel timers, each with a small button above it to be pressed by a player after a move. This stops player time and starts opponent time. This simplified device enabled a player to survive severe time trouble, situations where it was necessary to make 20 or 30 movements with less than one minute remaining. The next big reform, the inclusion of a tiny latch called a flag, occurred at the turn of the 19th century and helped end the chronic arguments about whether a player met a time limit. Lying straight down at the top of a clock face, the flag is lifted by the minute hand at the end of an hour until it is perpendicular and then falls straight down again. Until the flag was introduced, an arbiter or judge had to determine whether the minute hand passed 12. No further changes were made until digital clocks appeared in the 1980s. Digital clocks tell the second player exactly how much time remains, but players have not proved popular.

Standard controls

The first controls implemented in 1861 were 24 moves in two hours, and most games were done in five hours. However, as defensive skills advanced, a game's total period of moves increased, and 24 moves in two hours proved overly forgiving. At the 1862 London tournament, more than a fifth of the deciding games ended with step 30. This number dropped to 21% at Vienna 1873, 18% at Leipzig 1894, and less than 10% at Carlsbad 1923.

When players developed more thorough opening preparation—and could memorize a game's first 20 moves—the pressure for quicker limits intensified. A format of 30 moves in two hours became popular by the 1880s, followed by 36 moves in two hours in the 1920s, then 40 moves in two and a half hours after World War II. In major events, a game was normally adjourned after the first five-hour play session and continued later. Critics said this offered an unnecessary opportunity to consult friends, seconds, or even machines after 1980.

A new format in the mid-1980s, 40 moves in two hours followed by a second time regulation of 20 moves in one hour, proved common because few games lasted beyond 60 moves and thus few needed adjournment. Many amateur events introduced a changed form of sudden-death clause to help prevent adjournments: after second or third time control was achieved, players were given an extra period of time usually an hour, to complete all their remaining moves. This was primarily used in nonmaster events, but it was also introduced in the Professional Chess Association championship in 1995.

Quick chess

Early chess clocks also fail after prolonged use. Sturdier clocks, emerging after World War I, made a modern style of casual chess possible, played at incredibly fast speeds, such as five-minute sudden-death games, which proved to be extremely common among younger players.

However, until the 1980s, there was a strong difference in most players' minds between serious chess, played at slower controls with a time budget of two or three hours and additional time after each control was achieved and easy chess, based on a limited amount of allocated time and no additional time. The widespread adoption of sudden-death controls in the 1980s after the first four or five hours of play proved a bridge between serious and rapid chess. The most famous modern model in the mid-1980s limited a whole game to 25 minutes per player. This power, called action chess, active chess, quick play, and game/25, became popular as it offered a livelier tempo with which a whole tournament could be completed in an evening.

Moreover the tempo adjustment did not seem to change relative play capabilities. Anatoly Karpov, a former world champion at slower pace and the highest-rated player in the event, won the first world fast championship in Mexico in 1988. The PCA arranged a 4-game/25 tourney circuit called the Grand Prix in 1994. Overall winners in their first two years were Vladimir Kramnik, the third-highest-rated player in the world, and Gary Kasparov, the PCA champion and the world's top-rated player. An example of how well-accepted the faster time limit is was FIDE's adoption to break ties in some important events. For example, in 1988, a first-round match between Canada's Kevin Spraggett and Soviet Union's Andrei Sokolov in the candidates' elimination matches leading to the world championship was tied after eight games and determined when Spraggett won a game/15 tiebreaker.

The Fisher clock

In the 1990s, Fast Chess took a new turn with variation on Staunton's single-move theory and Lasa's time-budget concept. Fischer, who had not played a public game after winning the 1972 World Championship, invented a 1988 chess clock that introduced more time after a player completed a move and pressed the button on top. For example, a player could start with five minutes in a speed game and receive 10 or 15 seconds after each move.

The Fischer clock received international recognition after the expatriate American came out of retirement in 1992 for a non-sanctioned World Championship match with Boris Spassky in Belgrade and Sveti Stefan in Yugoslavia. The match rules stipulated that each player start 111 minutes on his clock and earn one minute for each move made. This meant that each player had been given 151 minutes, or one minute more than the 40-in-2 1/2-hour format used when Fischer won the Spassky championship title in 1972. For the second power, the match rules gave each player an additional 40 minutes to play 20 moves, but included an extra minute for each played move. As chess promoters moved towards arranging spectator tournaments—especially television audiences—in mind, shorter time limits became a lifestyle for professional players. One of the most fascinating annual tournaments, held since 1992 in Monaco, features top grandmasters playing a pair of games using the Fischer clock. In one of the games, players start four minutes and earn 10 seconds for each move made. In the second, they play the board without sight—so-called blindfold chess—beginning with four minutes and earning 20 seconds per pass.

BIBLIOGRAPHY

"Recognized Sports Federations: World Chess Federation". International Olympic Committee. Archived from the original on 23 October 2017. Retrieved 10 December 2020.

"Fide Laws of Chess taking effect from 1 January 2018". FIDE. Retrieved 10 December 2020.

United States Chess Federation. (2003). U.S. Chess Federation's official rules of chess. Just, Tim., Burg, Daniel B. (5th ed.). New York. ISBN 0-8129-3559-4. OCLC 52859422.

"Louis Charles Mahe De La Bourdonnais". Chessgames.com. Archived from the original on 29 December 2008. Retrieved 10 December 2020.

Bird, Henry Edward (January 2004). Chess History and Reminiscences. Gutenberg. Archived from the original on 24 September 2009. Retrieved 10 December 2020.

René Gralla (19 November 2006). "XiangQi – an alternate to Western Chess". ChessBase.com. Archived from the original on 4 June 2011.

Harkness, Kenneth (1967), Official Chess Handbook, McKay

Hooper, David; Whyld, Kenneth (1996) [First pub. 1992], The Oxford Companion to Chess (2nd ed.), Oxford University Press, ISBN 0-19-280049-3

Just, Tim (2014), U.S. Chess Federation's Official Rules of Chess (6th ed.), McKay, ISBN 978-0-8129-3559-2

Polgar, Susan; Truong, Paul (2005), A World Champion's Guide to Chess, Random House, ISBN 978-0-8129-3653-7

Reinfeld, Fred (1954), How To Be A Winner At Chess, Fawcett, ISBN 0-449-91206-X

Ruch, Eric (2004), The Italian Rules, ICCF, Retrieved 10 December 2020

Schiller, Eric (2003), Official Rules of Chess (2nd ed.), Cardoza, ISBN 978-1-58042-092-1

Staunton, Howard (1847), The Chess-Player's Handbook, London: H. G. Bohn, pp. 21–22, ISBN 0-7134-5056-8 (1985 Batsford reprint, ISBN 1-85958-005-X)

Sunnucks, Anne (1970), The Encyclopaedia of Chess, St. Martin's Press (2nd ed.), ISBN 978-0-7091-4697-1

Timman, Jan (2005), Curaçao 1962: The Battle of Minds that Shook the Chess World, New in Chess, ISBN 978-90-5691-139-3

www.ingramcontent.com/pod-product-compliance
Lightning Source LLC
Chambersburg PA
CBHW070626220526
45466CB00001B/104